TRADDY DADDY

The author, drawn by his son

Traddy Daddy

❧

MEMORIES AND THOUGHTS
OF THE FATHER OF
A CATHOLIC FAMILY

JOSEPH BEVAN

Foreword by
BISHOP ATHANASIUS SCHNEIDER

Copyright © 2025 Joseph Bevan
All rights reserved.

No part of this book may be reproduced, stored in a retrieval system, or transmitted in any form, or by any means, electronic, mechanical, photocopying, or otherwise, without the prior written permission of the publisher, except by a reviewer, who may quote brief passages in a review.

Os Justi Press
P.O. Box 21814
Lincoln, NE 68542
www.osjustipress.com

Send inquiries to
info@osjustipress.com

ISBN 978-1-965303-70-2 (paperback)
ISBN 978-1-965303-72-6 (hardcover)
ISBN 978-1-965303-73-3 (ebook)

Layout by Michael Schrauzer
Cover by Julian Kwasniewski
Cover image: Norman Rockwell, "What Fathers Know Best"

CONTENTS

	Foreword. ix	
	Preface. xi	
CHAPTER 1	Emergence. 1	
CHAPTER 2	All Change. 11	
CHAPTER 3	Battles 16	
CHAPTER 4	Against the Odds 27	
CHAPTER 5	Turning the Screw 44	
CHAPTER 6	My Apostasy. 59	
CHAPTER 7	Growing Pains. 79	
CHAPTER 8	A Very Common Story 83	
CHAPTER 9	Life on the Farm 98	
CHAPTER 10	Life Under Fire 107	
CHAPTER 11	Working It Out 124	
CHAPTER 12	How to Protect Children. 138	
CHAPTER 13	First Fruits. 149	
CHAPTER 14	Health Issues and Other Turmoils 175	
CHAPTER 15	"Something Rotten in the State of Denmark". 192	
CHAPTER 16	Confusion Reigns. 201	
CHAPTER 17	The Elusive Peace. 218	
	Epilogue 229	

FOREWORD

JOSEPH BEVAN DESCRIBES IN TRADDY *Daddy* many basic aspects in his full, busy, and eventful life. He was a member of a musical family of fourteen, himself the father of a family of ten children and an active and campaigning adherent to the cause of Catholic Tradition. Finally, he stakes his claim as a Catholic writer, who demonstrates his own worldview concerning the obvious moral and social crises in the world. In this latter role he has had many essays published in the Catholic press.

Having much enjoyed reading Joseph's previous book *Two Families*, which was published in July 2024, I was left with unanswered questions, wanting to find out more about his life, especially concerning his upbringing and his (and his family's) experiences when dealing with the religious upheavals of the 1960s and 1970s. Having had a preview of *Traddy Daddy*, I am not disappointed. It is also splendid to read his accounts of managing the upbringing of his ten children along with his excellent wife, Clare. The arrival of three vocations, two priests and a nun, as well as the perseverance of the other seven children in the Faith, show the effectiveness of their efforts with the help of God's grace. Reading *Traddy Daddy*, one can see how a simple life of prayer and the reception of the sacraments has been repaid by God a hundredfold. That is the real message of *Traddy Daddy*: God did it all.

The book is written in the present tense, which is certainly brave and courageous, and not without its risks. I am pleased to report that Joseph succeeds in this project as he allows the reader to be a fellow traveller, allowing a certain intimacy between the writer and the reader. The events he recounts about the suffering of Catholics during and after Vatican II should be kept alive, and this book is a timely rebuttal to those who wish to play down the existence of such sufferings.

We thank Joseph Bevan for this enthralling book, which demonstrates the treasure of the holy, unchanging, and beautiful Catholic Faith, lived and transmitted, amidst trials but also joys, in a Catholic family. And that is what really counts in the end.

August 15, 2025
Feast of the Assumption of Our Lady

✣ ATHANASIUS SCHNEIDER
Auxiliary Bishop of the Archdiocese
of Saint Mary in Astana

PREFACE

OPINIONS ON MY LAST BOOK, TWO *Families*, published in July 2024, were varied, but I did notice a demand for "more of the same." I realise that the previous book also attracted comments such as "harsh," "brutal," "unnecessarily critical," and, in some cases, there was a bad reaction on the part of those of my immediate family who objected to seeing their names in print.

For this I must apologise, but fact is often stranger than fiction and the events described would have been barely believable had I not kept to the genuine facts and named people who really existed. Had I disguised the characters, the book would have been regarded as the product of a rather fertile imagination and would have been consigned to oblivion. Also, I did not betray any confidences or let out any family secrets, as the facts which I set down are well known, and by no means unique to my family. To those of my family who are still not reconciled to my previous book and feel offended, I can only say that my affection for them is undiminished and I wouldn't dream of ascribing to them motives which are in any way dishonourable. That would be utterly wrong of me. After all, we are all victims of the maelstrom which surrounds the current moral order and, thanks to the worsening plight of the Catholic Church, we are all like sheep without a shepherd.

In my full and eventful life, much has happened that was omitted in *Two Families*, and so the purpose of this volume is to fill in the gaps and provide my readers with a more complete picture. In addition, I hope I do not try the readers' patience by analysing, so far as I am able, certain issues which surround the bringing up of children and also those connected with the crisis into which the family, the Catholic Church, society, and the world at large, are now plunged.

Traddy Daddy is written largely in the present tense, and this is designed to place the readers in the middle of the events as they are described and to allow them to accompany me on a journey. As these vicissitudes are set out, so also are my accompanying thoughts, and the reader is completely free to disagree with my reactions and form his own.

For those readers who are rash enough to read this volume to the last page, the question might be asked: Who cares what Joseph Bevan thinks? This reaction may be justified, and I have given it much thought. I can only say this in reply. My thoughts and opinions are intended to approach human affairs from a purely supernatural point of view. For example, I do not suggest a magic answer to the interminable problems described in the media outlets, nor am I qualified to do so. I suppose I am supplying an analysis which would have been commonplace in the centuries when the Church was in its right mind. As I state on numerous occasions, I am personally and arbitrarily convinced that our lives are eighty percent supernatural and twenty percent human, and this is the key which unlocks

Preface xiii

so many of the dilemmas which we face. As I am not qualified in theology or philosophy at all, I hope my readers will forgive me if I stray into areas which do not stand up to close examination. I am assured by my children, though, that this book is remarkably free from error!

I take this opportunity to give heartfelt thanks to my longsuffering wife, Clare, for all the help and advice she has given me. Clare is my most valued critic and confidante, for without her this volume may well have turned out to be completely disorganised, incoherent, and probably libellous. I am also most grateful to Mr Henry Sire for putting me right on Elizabethan history.

Many of the characters mentioned here are dead and, as they are mainly baptized Catholics, I pray for them and pray to them, assuming that they are now suffering souls in purgatory. May they pray for me also.

A few linguistic notes have been added for the benefit of American readers.

Joseph Bevan
Dover
Pentecost 2025

CHAPTER 1

Emergence

1966: WESTMINSTER CATHEDRAL CHOIR SCHOOL

The priest mutters his way through the Latin prayers during early morning Mass as we boys kneel in adoration in the dusty half-light of the crypt under Westminster Cathedral. The celebrant stands at the altar with his back to us as he performs the work of a master craftsman, and he whispers the prayers. I look up during the elevation of the host and watch the fishes in the mosaic depicted on the arch above the altar, as I have done hundreds of times before. There is Our Lord walking on the water and there's the ship containing the apostles who are scared by the storm. Fish abound in the picture, and I try to count them. Having had nothing to eat I often feel faint at the priest's recitation of the *Agnus Dei*, during which he bends slightly and taps his chest three times. Why I do so at that particular time of the Mass I have no idea and today I pass out momentarily.

Sister Immaculata frogmarches me out of the crypt and sends me on a trot around the car park outside. I find that attending Mass on a completely empty stomach is a bit of a trial, but, as it is Sunday, we do get a decent breakfast afterwards.

Nevertheless, I am struck by the dual simplicity and dignity of the ceremony, with the priest in sparkling gold vestments on Saints' days. To my young brain, the whole ceremony is rich with deep meaning which is beyond my comprehension, and represents the magnificence of the supreme orderliness which is the Catholic Church. Everything is in its place and the whole organisation reminds me of an ancient clock which ticks away over the centuries and never loses a beat. During the hush of the consecration of the host, I hear the low mumbling and tinkling bells of other Masses which are going on in the various crypt chapels. There is also the distant rumble of traffic in Victoria Street.

On Sundays we have crispy rolls for breakfast, which I look forward to all week, after which we shiver in the playground while one of the boys produces a model car to which Fr Comerford solemnly attaches a "Jettex" propellant capsule which he ignites with his matches (he is a pipe smoker). Soon the car whizzes around the playground and promptly bursts into flames to the accompaniment of wild cheering. Then the cathedral choir boys go off for their pre-High Mass rehearsal in the song school and my two elder brothers, Tony and Rupert, are among them. I am too young for the cathedral choir, having just joined the school, and am designated a probationer. Roger Pugh teaches singing to us probationers and encourages us to make the same noise, when singing, as we do when we run around in the playground. We oblige, and the result is the finest choir in Europe.

Every Sunday we wear our smartest uniforms as we file into the cathedral for High Mass and take our places in the front two rows facing the grand altar. The interior of the church is constructed out of miniature red bricks, reminding me of Legos and, for a little boy of my size, it's vast. I cannot see the roof as it soars up above my head shrouded in darkness. Above the high altar is a decorative baldacchino which, to me, is as big as a railway bridge, and hanging over the sanctuary a massive crucifix keeps sentinel over the proceedings. The organ is growling in the background as the church begins to fill up. Some people kneel whilst reciting their rosaries and knots of people cluster around the votive candle stations as they light candles and kneel in prayer. No one is talking and all I can hear is the shuffling of many feet and the creaking of chairs as they quietly take their places with the organ playing in the background. Sister Immaculata fusses over us like a mother hen and ensures that we have our missals open at the correct page. My own Mass book contains a section at the end of the service called "post communion" and I have concluded that it is for when the priest posts off holy communion to people who have been unable to attend.

SOLEMN HIGH MASS IN THE CATHEDRAL

When Cardinal Heenan arrives at the door of the Church, he is met by the most senior canon. The bells are rung. The organist releases the swell pedal a little to warn the crowd that things are starting to happen; they stand up. The canon offers the Cardinal some holy water with which he crosses himself and sprinkles a little on the assembled company of clergy. He is wearing a rochet, a cappa magna, a long dark red cloak which trails along the floor, and which is held up by attendants, and a biretta, which is a red upside-down strawberry punnet with a silk tassel.

Accompanied by the attendants who carry his train, the cardinal visits the chapel of the Blessed Sacrament and there, kneeling at the altar, he makes a short prayer. Then he comes in procession to the high altar and, as he progresses, he blesses the celebrant and other ministers who kneel to receive his benediction. Eventually he goes to his throne, which is against the wall to the left of the altar, the gospel side. The throne is magnificently decorated in the liturgical colours of the day including the coat of arms of the prelate emblazoned on a shield which is suspended above. He takes off his biretta and cappa magna while the servers bring the vestments from the altar. The deacons at the throne assist the cardinal to put these on. Finally, a deacon puts the mitre on the cardinal's head. His Eminence holds the crozier in his left hand and goes to the altar, blessing the clergy as he passes.

When the cardinal arrives before the altar steps to begin Mass he gives the crozier to its bearer, the second deacon takes off the mitre and all reverence the altar. Meanwhile the celebrant of the Mass comes to the altar with his ministers; he stands at the cardinal's left before the steps, a little back. The deacons of the throne stand behind the cardinal, the deacon and subdeacon of the Mass stand to the left of the celebrant and a little behind him.

The other chaplains or servers of the cardinal are positioned behind these.

The first Master of Ceremonies (MC) is on the Epistle (right hand) side, the second MC on the Gospel side. The trainbearer stands on the Epistle side. All except the Cardinal and the celebrant and canons kneel. The Cardinal and celebrant start the prayers at the foot of the altar, *Introibo ad altare Dei*, the celebrant answering the cardinal, *ad Deum qui laetificat juventutem meum*. And so, the Mass gets underway while the congregation look on in wonder at this beautifully choreographed liturgy, much of it dating back to the Roman catacombs. It all happens to the accompaniment of ancient Gregorian chant and sublime polyphonic music from the rich treasures of the Renaissance, sung by the choir.

The Mass comes to an end and the Cardinal processes out, blessing the people left and right and smiling broadly, his silver spectacles glinting in the candlelight. The Cardinal's chaplain is standing just behind him, also grinning broadly. Sister Immaculata makes us stay on for a few minutes to allow the bulk of the congregation to leave and also so that we may say a quick thanksgiving. As we file into the school refectory for lunch a little later there are gasps from the boys as they observe a box of chocolates on each of our dining tables, presumably a gift from a well-wisher. On a raised platform is a table for Father Veal, the headmaster, Father Comerford, the assistant Head, and any guests. As it is a Sunday there are a few of those and they drink wine, but we do not. Father Veal has a little handbell which he rings when he gives us permission to talk during meals. He also rings it when he requires us to be quiet. On bad days we never hear the bell, so we eat in silence and observe the gloom on the high table. At lunch one Sunday, Father Veal turns on the radio as usual and we listen to the news, included in which is the statement that record numbers of people have just attended Mass in Westminster Cathedral.

SCHOOL LIFE

My favourite service in the cathedral is Sunday Vespers. Again, we probationers occupy the front two rows and follow the service in our missals. The psalms at Vespers move me to tears sometimes; even as a boy of eight my sensitivity is acute, and I am transported by the sight of five priests in gold copes among the clouds of incense. During the incensing, while the altar is prepared for Benediction of the Blessed Sacrament, the organist plays thunderously and it is this part of the ceremony that I look forward to most of all, for the organist is Nicholas Kynaston who, we are told, is internationally famous.

We have to go to confession once a week, and for this we again visit the cathedral. Confessional boxes are dotted all over the church, but there is one particular confessional box at the back, up against a pillar. That is where Father Veal, our headmaster, hears confessions. We all queue up for that one despite the availability of at least ten other confessional boxes. Simon Morgan, a boy in my class, collects up some mosaic tiles which are left in a pile in one of the side chapels, and he makes a human figure out of plasticine and decorates it with the pilfered contraband. Father Veal had warned us all sternly about removing mosaic tiles from the church and Morgan knows this but, nevertheless, he foolishly shows his work of art to Sister Immaculata who praises it to the heavens and sends him to Father Veal to show him also. This he is very reluctant to do, but, regardless, he bravely knocks on Father's door and goes in. Father very splendidly guesses what has happened and tells Morgan off lightly, with tongue in cheek.

I am probably the most unpopular boy in the school because I am disagreeable, arrogant, and needlessly violent. I even attack boys who are twice my size and in doing so attract swift pugilistic retribution. On my birthday I am allowed to throw a tea party in the refectory which takes place at the same time as normal school tea on the other tables. I am permitted to invite my friends to this party but, having none, decide to buy some favour with the other boys. I therefore invite all my chief persecutors to the tea, and this causes raised eyebrows, although they are all grateful and a ceasefire ensues for a short while. One evening I am just about to close my eyes after "lights-out" and I feel somebody sitting on my bed; it is Father Veal. He gives me a severe and angry talking-to which is fatherlike and sincere. I promise to mend my aggressive ways, so the process of healing begins but I am taken away from this school before any lasting results are achieved.

Quite often Sister Immaculata takes us to the cathedral during the week to visit the Blessed Sacrament in a special chapel set aside for devotions. We follow the nun quietly through the echoing cathedral where we see people praying, strolling around, or lighting votive candles. The Blessed Sacrament chapel is off a side aisle to the left of the high altar and when we enter, we see many people kneeling down. Some are holding rosaries and whispering the prayers. The centre of devotional attention is the gold tabernacle on the altar, surrounded by lighted candles and flowers. I smell the sweet odour of the incense of past ceremonies, and the attendant hush is in striking contrast to the noisiness of the London traffic outside in Victoria Street. I have no difficulty in saying prayers as I am transported by the beauty of the chapel and the fervour of the people around me. My childlike approach to prayer, which has never left me, was formed during those wonderful visits to the cathedral.

One Wednesday afternoon we are milling around in the playground and Father Veal is walking around the perimeter of the lawn in the distance, buried in his breviary. All the priests I meet at the choir school, and there are lots of them, seem to have their daily lives dominated by this mysterious black prayer book which they always carry around with them. It is this same afternoon that I accidently kick a football into the distance, and it strikes Father Veal, causing him to stumble and drop his prayer book. He angrily escorts me to his study as this is the culmination of a series of unpunished annoyances which I have recently caused. He tells me to bend over and administers the gentlest of whacks with a sole of a shoe. I barely feel any pain but the emotional effect on me is devastating, and

I am inconsolable. The man to whom I give honour, love, and respect is cross with me and, as a result, I feel that I have betrayed his friendship.

Every evening, before bedtime, we assemble on the third floor of the school, the doors at the far end are opened before us, and we kneel down for prayers. A red lamp hangs down above the altar, to show us that the Blessed Sacrament is present, and Father Veal leads the night prayers which end with one of the four Marian hymns, depending on the liturgical season—either *Salve Regina*, *Regina Caeli*, *Ave Regina* or *Alma Redemptoris Mater*. Finally, Father gives us his blessing and off to bed we go. When we are ready to go to sleep Father reads to us and this is how I get to know the works of C. S. Lewis and Robert Louis Stevenson. During a reading of *Prince Caspian*, Father snaps the book shut, as he often does when things are getting exciting, and the whole school roars a protest from their beds. Shocked by this outrage, and not a little impressed, he reopens the book and continues reading for a while.

For some reason I am often ill; my medical records contain in the summary a single word, "tendency." The sick bay at the choir school is a single bedroom near the senior three classroom. The bed is very comfortable and I sleep well, thus accelerating my recovery from whatever illness I am suffering from. One night I am woken by a shuffling sound coming from the other bed, which is vacant. I sit up carefully in my bed and observe the figure of a nun kneeling in the dark at the other bed and obviously praying. I am not at all frightened, quite the reverse, as I am comforted by her presence. She does not reappear. I make enquiries when I'm discharged from the sick bay and draw a blank from Sister Immaculata and some other nuns whom I ask about the apparition. Was it a ghost? I have the certain feeling that it was, so I try not to be ill again as a repeat of the experience may terrify me.

We have religious instruction lessons with Father Veal, and he first distributes to each of us a little red booklet called the *Penny Catechism*. Over the next few terms, he makes us learn the whole thing parrot fashion and we recite sections of it back to him together in a singsong chorus. There is a lot of discussion, which Father leads and encourages, and in doing so he displays his own deep love of the Catholic Faith, which is infectious.

School outings are often arranged and, on one particular Wednesday after High Mass, the whole school of forty boys boards the train for a visit to Portsmouth Harbour. When we arrive at Portsmouth Father Veal tells us to look into the distance and there, on the horizon, we see the masts of HMS Victory. This visit to Nelson's flagship has a deep effect on me and I maintain an interest in naval history throughout my life. After the visit is over, mention is made of us all having lunch in a Chinese restaurant in Portsmouth. I overhear some boys discussing the compulsory use of chopsticks and, for no reason which I can fathom, I am utterly terrified by this prospect.

CHAPTER 2

All Change

HOME AND PARISH LIFE

Home for the Easter Holidays at last! We have just moved into Parsonage Farm and my little sister Helen volunteers to show me around our village of Croscombe. We leave the house, and I am holding her hand. "This way," she announces, and pulls me along the road. "Are you sure?" I answer. So, we walk and eventually we find ourselves surrounded by fields and woods, not a house in sight. The new house is in a state of chaos as builders are constructing a new kitchen, so my brother Rupert and I have to sleep in the sitting room.

Our parish church in Shepton Mallet is a converted hall and every Sunday it is full. There is a choir gallery which our family inhabits so as to sing the Mass, and Pa plays the organ for us. We sing Gregorian chant and a few simple motets. I detect trouble ahead as something Pa calls "Vatican Two" is casting a shadow over everything religious. Attending Mass, after the experience of Westminster in term time, comes as a surprise but I am thoroughly entertained by the upheavals. Father Ryan is now facing us, having put in place a table which he uses as an altar. He is given to interrupting the service every so often to emit what Pa calls "sermonettes." Worst of all, we are forced to join in with the server in a rather wordy and tedious translation of the Latin Mass. Jokes abound with the cack-handed words, such as, "mindful of our Saviour's bidding, and for the *prairie tortoise*" (prayer he taught us).

Pa and my elder brothers, especially, are often angry after Mass. This is a massive alteration in our religious observance as respect for the parish priest, who is agitating for change, diminishes. I hear them mutter in annoyance when the priest gives an extra-long sermon about the "presidential chair," whatever that is. The whole of Mass is, for me at least, an orgy of experimentation and I look forward to each Sunday in anticipation of new outrages. Rather than being a servant of the liturgy, Father Ryan is behaving like a compère at a village dance, not resisting the odd joke or two either. Yet I am struck by the "do this or else" attitude of the priest, meaning that by taking our part in the changes we are being loyal subjects of the Holy Father. Nobody dares to object publicly, but privately people are either angry or mystified. Ma is convinced that the Pope has been kidnapped and is trussed up in a cellar in the Vatican. "Don't worry," she says, "he'll restore things to what they were after he escapes." This is how many people cling to hope.

At about this time we abandon the old chapel of St Nicholas and take possession of our new gleaming concrete and glass building which is St Michael's Church. As we enter the new building for the first time, I am immediately aware of that smell common to new buildings, it is the slightly sweet odour of floor polish. The altar is a slab of white bare stone and, unlike its predecessor at our last chapel, has no coverings. Also gone are the statues and the stations of the cross. The servers at Mass have abandoned their black cassocks and white cottas in favour of what look, to me at least, like long dresses which are coloured dark green.

With the new church comes a new parish priest, called Father Gerald Carrol, who has a string of drink-driving convictions, so we are told. I am under the impression that Father Carrol is a "conservative" (the Catholic Church nowadays is reduced to political name-calling) and is resisting pressure from some of the more enlightened members of his congregation to get rid of our family choir which sings for him every Sunday. I can only describe the goings-on at the altar during Mass as chaotic. Father Carrol is often not particularly sober and keeps on breaking out into Latin. The servers bustle around like headless chickens and constantly trip up over their green dresses which are far too long for some or far too short for others. The master of ceremonies pushes and shoves to restore some kind of order. As I am at a delicate age, I find all this tremendous fun, but I catch the sighs, the groans and sharp intakes of breath from those around me. During Mass of Low Sunday, we look up to see Father Carrol's little white dog entering the church through the open vestry door and, neglecting to genuflect, waddling past the front row of pews, and then settling down in the corner by the little organ. Mass continues normally but during the hymn at the offertory the dog starts to howl, so a parishioner picks it up and returns it to the vestry.

THE FAMILY CHOIR

The family choir is booked to give a concert in St Thomas's Church in Wells on the Saturday after Easter as part of the local music festival. There is a fee, but Pa isn't sure how much each of us will get as our share until he has defrayed his expenses. We are assured that the church will be full of people and, in any case, by this time our choir has gained a loyal following of admirers who never miss out on our concerts. The point being that the more people who turn up to listen, the bigger the fee. The choir at the moment consists of nine of the Bevan children and offers a wide range of compositions but, by a long mile, the preferred music is that of the polyphonic composers of the sixteenth century. As it is Easter, Pa includes in the programme some Holy Week responsories composed by Victoria, which are especially loved by the children. There are also some Welsh folk songs which have been arranged by Pa. These are not liked and are rather difficult as there are a series of complicated repeats which my sister Rachel, in particular, gets into a muddle over.

The choir possesses several remarkable gifts, one being the ability, come what may, to stay in tune, not only with each other, but also with the correct key. Another gift is the ability, whatever goes wrong, to make it sound as though the piece is *supposed* to go like that. After an embarrassing rendition of Thomas Tomkins's "When David heard" in Ludlow church, when everything that could possibly go wrong did go wrong, a member of the audience said afterwards that it was the highlight of the evening. Even our family friends in the audience didn't notice anything amiss. This calm and professional approach does not extend to the conductor, however, who flaps his arms around in a panic. But the choir members ignore their father as the train is calmly put back on the rails. It is noticeable that the choir does sometimes have problems with keeping time and this is attributed largely to Pa's method of conducting, which reminds people of the action when stirring treacle.

During the week after the Wells concert the younger children keep a weather eye out for the postman as they eagerly await the arrival of the fee cheque. When it finally arrives and each singer is rewarded in accordance with age, I receive the princely sum of one pound and ten shillings which represents riches indeed. I catch a bus to town with my younger brother Jeremy, similarly rewarded, and we make for the "trick shop" where we blow our hard-earned fee on bangers, catapults, exploding cigarettes, and whoopee cushions. These are necessities if one is to survive in a large family.

CHAPTER 3

Battles

1969: MY PREP SCHOOL

In one of his essays, George Orwell describes how, when he was a child, all grownups appeared ugly to him. This was because, being short, he would look up at adult men and all he could see were protruding hairy nostrils. He might have added that they mostly stank of pipe smoke and, at my prep school, were mainly hostile to us children, as the milk of human kindness was in short supply.

I am sent by my parents to All Hallows School near Shepton Mallet as a day pupil and receive daily lifts from Peter Scotland, the French master and head of games. Scotland isn't a bad chap really and seems to like us boys, which is a respite from some of the other teachers who obviously do not. In spite of him carting me to and from school every day, purely as a favour to Pa and out of the goodness of his heart, I am ashamed to say that I fool around during his French classes, for if anyone can kill off any possible enthusiasm for his subject, it's Scotland. No attempt is made at a French accent, and I often imagine him during the last war as a commando serving in France, which he was, yelling at waiters in Paris. It seems as though most of his French is learned from the phrase book issued to all soldiers before the invasion of Normandy. He has the use of a "teaching aid" during our lessons which is a projector and a screen linked to a tape recorder. A picture is shown on the screen of a commonplace French scene, such as children sitting around reading books. The tape machine announces the first picture, "Alice lit, Josette regarde la fenêtre." The tape is stopped, and Scotland asks, "Bevan, que fait Alice?" Upon receiving a satisfactory answer, he turns the reel of the film on the projector, *squeak-squeak*, and the tape machine intones the next picture. "Voici le chien, Meoux" echoes around the classroom whilst the boys fidget with boredom.

I never learn much French and my progress in this subject, and indeed, all the other subjects, is a matter of supreme indifference to the school authorities. I am placed, therefore, in the "B" stream for all subjects. The "A" stream is full of bright kids who are being groomed for scholarships to public school and have the best teachers. We in "B" stream, on the other hand, are simply marking time as they have more or less given up on us. I also labour under an additional disadvantage, which is that I have spent my two previous years at Croscombe Primary School, and I arrive at All Hallows knowing absolutely nothing. I am completely at sea in all the subjects, not having received any grounding in any of them. The main effect of this disability is that I am prone to ill-discipline and bad behaviour in class; not all classes, of course, as some of the masters are not to be trifled with, and yet they still teach me nothing. My lack of academic achievement is also not a worry to me, for my overriding sentiment at that school is one of fear: fear of a savage beating, fear of being bawled at, and fear of being beaten up by other boys, which happens a lot. It's this sense of dread which turns me into a nervous wreck who spends his school days keeping out of trouble and counting the minutes until he can slide with relief into the back of Mr Scotland's car for the ride home.

Upon arrival at home every evening I try to put school out of my mind and blank out the day's events. Completion of the mountain of homework which I have been set is out of the question and this is another way by which I store up more trouble for myself. Upon arrival at home, I eat high tea with my younger brothers and sisters and then I walk down to granny's cottage and slump in front of her television.

PREP SCHOOL UPHEAVALS

The headmaster of our school is what I can only describe as a humourless, steely, and alcohol-soaked child-hater and it is he who implements the changes in Catholic practice and liturgy following the Second Vatican Council. 1969 finds the Church in a maelstrom of chaos, upheaval, and experimentation. All Hallows, an unknown prep school in the middle of nowhere, is not immune to these revolutionary forces and Alistair Mortimer, our Headmaster, willingly carries the banner of progress. The school chapel, for example, a beautiful cruciform and ancient room with a remarkable reredos, is the first place to receive unwelcome attention from the reforming Headmaster. The altar is torn from its mountings and dragged out, leaving a space behind it from which the priest can face the congregation. The delicately carved wooden reredos is sold off, and a yellow curtain replaces it. The stations of the cross are removed along with the many statues of Our Lady, Saint Joseph, and the saints. A public address system is installed which often either breaks down or emits loud crackles which are extremely offensive to the ear.

This assault on the school chapel has the effect of undermining the Catholicity of the whole school. It reminds one of a mischievous engineer sabotaging the engine of a ship. Now, I have no doubt that our headmaster is acting on orders from above and feels that he has no choice but to implement the changes, and yet his energetic zeal in carrying them out is, I think, beyond the call of duty. He's not alone, as the same things are going on in almost every Catholic institution in the world and the enthusiasm with which the destruction is carried out must have surprised the Church authorities who may have anticipated at least some resistance. The traditional Latin Mass is swept away also and replaced by what my family describe as a "hymn-burger," that is, an English Mass with a hymn at the beginning and the end with one stuck in the middle for good measure.[1] The Latin Mass, which provided the spiritual heart and soul of the school, is now replaced by a turgid and boring communion service which slowly but surely kills off any supernatural

---

[1] In the United States, apparently they call this a "four-hymn sandwich": processional or opening, offertory, communion, and recessional or closing.

love amongst the pupils. In fact, religion is now a tiresome chore.

There is a side entrance to the school chapel opening onto stone steps leading down to the school yard. A builders' skip[2] is parked near the steps and we boys observe workmen, supervised by Mortimer, energetically chucking some of the chapel contents into it: statues, pews, vestments, altar cloths, and box after box of prayer books and missals. After this we never see *A Simple Prayer Book* or *Plainsong for Schools* ever again. Thus, the centrepiece of the school is consigned to the builders' skip.

Like all private Catholic schools today, All Hallows offers an education to the children of any parents who are prepared to pay the ever-increasing school fees. The teaching of the catechism and the development of piety is exchanged for brutal academic success, and this is why many pupils fall by the wayside. In 1968 there's no formal Catholic teaching at all and the majority of the schoolmasters are non-Catholics, many of whom are ex-army officers. A monk from nearby Downside Abbey appears occasionally but his RI[3] classes are few and far between, and during them everything is discussed, apart from religion, of course.

During one of these lessons one afternoon, the monk, Dom Edmund, calls out to the front a boy called Hoskins and punches him hard in the stomach. The boy doubles up in pain and vomits onto the floor. One of the effects of the abandonment of the true Catholic religion, and the peace and

---

2 In the U. S., a dumpster.
3 Religious Instruction.

tranquillity which comes with it, is that violence of every type and description is a daily occurrence in the school, to the extent that few notice it as it is so common. The beatings administered by the headmaster are organised almost on an industrial level, with whole dormitories of perhaps thirty boys lining up and shivering in the early morning frost outside his study for what is known as a "whacking." He is a very large and powerful man and can, and does, inflict quite serious injury on his victims, to the extent that one boy, by the name of Farmer, is hospitalised. I still cannot fathom how this individual gets away with it and all I know is that his activities eventually become too much for the Abbot of Downside, the chairman of governors, who summons the headmaster to a meeting, but so far as I am aware, nothing happens to him.

The punishment system operating in the school is two-tier. First, there are "stripes," where the teacher writes out a short note containing the complaint about me which I am obliged to show to the headmaster. Depending on his mood he could either give me the thrashing of my life, or else he could allocate some task or other. The psychological torture which I undergo having received one of these "stripes" is so intense that my sense of self-preservation kicks in and I fold up the piece of paper and stuff it into my trouser pocket. For the remaining six weeks of the summer term, I scrupulously avoid encountering either the master who gave me the stripe, Colonel Yule, or the headmaster himself. A week later Mr Quin, the science master, asks me whether I had taken the stripe to the headmaster yet. My mini-rebellion must have become common knowledge in the staff room by now because, in the history of the school, I believe that nobody, but nobody, had refused to "go for the stripe." After much anguish and near fatal encounters with the master concerned, I arrive home for the summer holidays. With a feeling of intense joy and relief, I retrieve the offending paper from my trouser pocket and, despite the fact that it has almost disintegrated, I tear it up into little pieces and flush them down the outside lavatory.

The secondary system of punishments is the "drill" system. If you are awarded a "drill" for an allegedly minor misdemeanour, the offence will be logged in the drill book and the offenders have to assemble before morning lessons, rain or shine, outside the front of the school. A prefect then makes the miscreants perform a set number of drills such as squat jumps and press-ups. Fortunately, it is a prefect who supervises this punishment, and, on the whole, the prefects aren't such a bad lot, as they are really suffering from the injustices of the system as much as we are. When I am obliged, towards the end of the Lent term, to attend drill for some refraction or other, the exercises are interrupted by the arrival of Colonel Yule, pipe in mouth, who proceeds to drill us to exhaustion. Many of the boys, me included, are unable to stand up after it is over. The drill book is an evil publication and at school line-up every day, armed with it, the headmaster reads out the drills awarded on the previous day. Prefects are allowed to award drills but not stripes.

One morning we are standing as usual in the colonnade and the headmaster is reading out the drills. "Watson, two drills, for going around with his hands in his pockets, Mason, one drill for dropping litter. Giles, two drills for whistling at an assistant matron." There is a pause, everyone looks up. "Giles!" roars the headmaster, "come to my study *this instant!*" Poor Giles, he is a regular feature in the drill book and his bottom must be made of cowhide given the regular and almost daily assaults on it. Nevertheless, he seems to laugh the whole thing off and I remember, over fifty years later, his indomitable spirit and cheerful disposition. He would have made an excellent bishop!

A BAD EXPERIENCE

One morning it is announced that there's going to be a rehearsal for the forthcoming school photograph. We are told to assemble in the large classroom that evening, much to my annoyance, as I normally go home by then. I have to use the staff room telephone to call my family to say that I will be home late. Interestingly it is insisted that a master, Schutz, has to be standing next to me while I telephone and has to listen in to everything I say. I find that most odd. After supper we all file to the large classroom: it is a tight fit as there are over one hundred and fifty boys standing shoulder to shoulder, there not really being enough room for us all. The headmaster enters looking flushed and, as soon as he opens his mouth, I know that he's intoxicated. His leery slobbering face comes up close to us and we can all smell the sour and sickly odour which begins to fill the room. The practice for the school photograph is a farce as the headmaster drunkenly orders people to stand in a certain place. We are all utterly confused and unsure about what the point of this gathering is.

"Stand there. Not there! Farquesson you big dodo, wake up!" shouts the headmaster as the room becomes a melee of confused boys bumping into each other.

"What's the matter with Farquesson?" he inquires. The boy is crying quietly into his sleeve. "Isn't dodo going to answer? Anybody!?" he shouts.

Lomax answers hesitantly, "you keep calling him a dodo, sir, and he's very upset about it."

At this, the headmaster calls out, "Farquesson—you're not a boy, you're a girl. Walker," addressing the head boy, "go down to my study and fetch my cane." The rest of the evening is a nightmare of crying and shrieking boys: I think at least twenty of them get thrashed in front of the whole assembly. Normally the punishment is limited to three strokes of the cane, but this man is savagely striking certain boys repeatedly, six or eight strokes, and for what reason? In my terrified confusion I hide under a table as this monster sets about his innocent victims with wild alcohol-induced vigour. After the ordeal is over, I observe the headmaster walking by himself across the schoolyard while taking long swigs out of a bottle.

Every Saturday, while most civilised schoolchildren have a day off, I am obliged to attend lessons in the morning and compelled to watch the first fifteen play another school at rugger during the afternoon, if there's a home match. We are all astonished one Saturday afternoon as we witness the visiting team kicking, biting, and scratching their way through the match. They lose, of course, and at the post-match tea they tell us that they face a beating from their headmaster as a reprisal for losing.

Father Carrol, the parish priest of Shepton Mallet and the chaplain to our school, arrives to celebrate benediction in the newly reordered chapel. He is clearly plastered, no doubt due to a good lunch, and when he kneels down in front of the altar in adoration, he sways this way and that so that the servers on either side of him, also kneeling, lean into his body to stop him toppling over. He mumbles the prayers and skips large parts of the service.

Seeing on the chapel notice board, *Jesus invites you to a dinner party in the Chapel on Sunday at 10am*, I mentally resolve to abandon all religion as soon as possible.

When I get up one Monday morning, I am so overwhelmed with the feeling of sickening dread that I try to knock myself unconscious by banging my head against my bedroom wall. This is because my mathematics teacher, Colonel Yule, reduces me to a quaking jelly simply by being in the same classroom as me. Redolent of stale pipe tobacco, he always wears the same patched sports jacket with corduroy trousers hitched up to his midriff by braces. Pipe in mouth, he scowls at us boys and I cannot imagine him ever smiling. The Colonel is my arch-tormentor because of his explosive temper. If any boy displeases him, he roars for five minutes and his bellowing echoes round the school buildings. Does this man have a wife? I ask myself. Does he have children? Does he know what it is to love or be loved? It is only an institution such as All Hallows that can provide a home for such a monster. He isn't a Catholic because I do not see him in chapel, not that it would make any difference because many of the practising Catholics on the teaching staff are just as evil. Take, for example, Olga Smith, a short and over-painted lady who wobbles around on high heels, clack-clacking as she goes. Olga teaches English and, like Yule, has a vile and volcanic temper. She has protruding front teeth onto which she accidently spills her bright red lipstick, and this conveys to me the impression of a vampire.

Some masters are kind, though, and bring an element of sanity into our trouble lives. Special mention should be made of Jim Blunt and Helmut Schutz. Both practising Catholics, they don't shout at us and their company provides us with a brief respite from the onslaught of their colleagues, whom I can only describe as child-haters. There is no one to whom we can go and state our true feelings, as even these two masters are regarded by us as very much part of the establishment—not that we would want to anyway because expressing one's true feelings, even if we are aware of such things, is "not done." True men don't "feel," we are told, they "think"! Even back home I never feel disposed to offload my reservoir of anxieties and dread to anyone. It never occurs to me. Why is this?

CHAPTER 4

Against the Odds

1970: THE BEVANS AT HOME

It is my last term at All Hallows and, on the twentieth of May, Pope Paul VI canonises the forty martyrs of England and Wales—brave men and women who, says the Holy Father, were "noble witnesses to human dignity and freedom." To celebrate this event the headmaster organises a day off lessons and a special lunch. After we had finished eating, Mortimer stood up in his place and asked if any boy could name one of the martyrs whose canonisations we were celebrating. This was met by universal silence, as none could.

The village of Croscombe nestles in the heart of the Mendip Hills and straddles the A30, a busy main road cluttered with slow moving tractors, between the twin towns of Shepton Mallet and Wells in Somerset. As you approach from Shepton Mallet you will see on the right the village primary school, where I was a pupil between leaving Westminster Cathedral and starting at All Hallows, and, on the left, there is a walled garden owned by Charlie Griffin, who spends all his time on his vegetables. Most days he is there, rain or shine, bent over his hoe as he expertly removes every weed. Griffin is on nodding terms with our family, but he's always puzzled by the strains of choral singing emanating from the large house which overlooks his garden. It is a Tuesday in the Easter holidays and at about eleven o'clock in the morning the sun has vanished behind a cloud and rain threatens. Not real rain, but a kind of annoying Scotch mist which pervades this part of the country and can go on for days. Charlie stands up straight to rest his back and, leaning on his rake, stares wistfully, first at the sky, and then at the house, and shakes his head. "What a useless load of toffs!" he growls. "Never done a day's work in their loives," he grumbles ill-naturedly. He then recalls with sadness how Parsonage Farm was once a working farm owned by his old friend Mrs Barrand who kept Border Collies; she has left the village for an old people's home. Roger Bevan has now moved in with his wife, Mollie, and their fourteen children, the youngest of whom, Ben, is a babe in arms.

Croscombe in 1970 is a thriving village which has two public houses, three grocery stores, and a post office. The church, which is just behind the "Rose and Crown," dates back to the fifteenth century and contains some of the finest examples of Jacobean pews in the country. It has a distinct pointed spire which can be seen for miles around. The local population consists mainly of farming families with names such as Gumbleton and Parfitt. They are still essentially folks who are wedded to the land—a land which slopes on either side, so it isn't suitable for crops. Sheep farming is mostly in evidence with some dairy herds which can be maintained on the plateaux. Many of the inhabitants have not travelled more than ten miles from home, and London or Bristol may as well be on the moon for all they know.

In front of the Rose and Crown is the ancient market cross where the thirstier villagers assemble and gossip, as they keep an ear open for the bolts of the public house front door, which are slid aside before they can file in for their first sleevers of cider top. A "sleever" is a long straight pint glass without a handle and a "cider top" is almost a pint of the cloudy yellow liquid made from apples, a drink so strong that even the hardened alcoholics have to top it up with lemonade. Everybody smokes and the bar ceiling is a distinct dark yellow caused by aeons of tar contamination. In the public bar the drinkers settle down to their favourite benches and sit silently as they nurse their drinks. Occasionally a voice calls out in indecipherable local dialect some observation and the others all nod and say, "aarrrh," before silence resumes. I wonder whether they have caught the meaning of the interruption as most outsiders would suspect that the Somerset dialect is as incomprehensible to the locals as it is to an untrained ear. Following a long pause, during which all attention concentrates on the rumble of farm vehicles outside, another voice speaks up and, listening closely to the remark, it sounds like, "Wha thee err poshos makin' a dim racket at Parsnip Farm, ammer?" It's the voice of Charlie Griffin who's sitting next to the inglenook fireplace and nursing his first pint of the morning after having given his weeds a good "seein' to." A few of the company look up from their drinks and agree, "aarrrh," and, with no one willing to develop the subject, it is quietly dropped.

For half an hour now, Pa is trying to conduct a rehearsal of the family choir in the music room of Parsonage Farm. It is a large square room with a low ceiling crisscrossed with huge black beams. The walls are stained with damp and in some places lumps of plaster have come away and lie in little piles on the floor. As the children, twelve of them, lounge around the grand piano clutching sheets of handwritten music, the atmosphere is one of irritation. Pa is sitting at the keyboard waving his right hand to beat time and playing broken chords as best he can, with the other.

A hectoring voice pipes up from the end of the piano, "Why do we suddenly have to sing this tosh?" It's Rachel, a singing student in London and home for the holidays. Rachel is the fifth eldest and dominates the soprano line with an effortless choirboy sound, much in vogue with the current revival of early music.

"Because," replies Pa with a sigh, "with the New Mass Father Carrol wants new music. I wrote these responsorial psalms myself and I thought they were rather good."

David, the fourth eldest and in his third year studying music at The Queen's College Oxford, interjects, "It's not the music, Pa, it's the words which are so trite and, well, *platitudinous.*"

"My goodness!," Rupert chimes in, "what long words we're using these days, David." Rupert, seventh in line, is in his penultimate year at Downside School, planning eventually to study horticulture at Pershore College. With his brother, John, the eldest in the family, he holds the bass line in the family choir.

"Do shut up, Rupert," snaps David, who continues, "I mean, telling God that he has the message of eternal life is quite ridiculous. Why does he need reminding?"

Tony enters the free-for-all. He is sixth in seniority, studying music at St John's College, Cambridge. He is by far the most pious of the children, so when he speaks his brothers and sisters listen rather than shouting him down, which is the usual treatment merited by his siblings. He begins politely, "well, David, I think God does rather need reminding because all these changes in the Mass must have confused him a little." This is received with much good-natured cackling by the rest of the family and even Pa breaks out into a smile.

"And what about this one?," continues David, "*Here I am, Lord, I come to do your will.* Who do these reformers think they are? The person who wrote that must be brain-dead! If they were meant to encourage participation, they're a complete flop. Nobody joins in. This is England after all."

Tony says, "and how about *O God, you are my God, for you my soul is searching.*" There is renewed laughter around the piano, a wheezy kind of laughter as many have varying degrees of asthma.

Cicely, alto, speaks for them all when she says, "I don't know about you lot but I'm not sure I can stand any more of these awful Masses." Her remark is greeted with an embarrassed silence, but Pa reacts angrily, "if you live at home you go to Mass!"

David says thoughtfully, "I don't think it's a question of giving up religion, it's just that we ought to find a priest who values our musical contribution and will carry on saying the Latin Mass, isn't that fair, Pa?"

"We have to obey the Holy Father," Pa replies. "We can't just walk away from our parish and find a church more to our liking, that was what we did in my Church of England days and one of the reasons why I became a Catholic in the first place."

"Hang on!," exclaims John, the eldest in the family. "Are you saying that it is better to give up religion completely than go to the Latin Mass?"

"I'm not saying anything more on the subject," says Pa, who has turned red. "Anyway, we still have to practise 'O quam gloriosum' for next Sunday's Mass."

"The knives are out for us in that church, even as we speak!," warns Tony.

WARFARE IN OUR PARISH

They are indeed! For that evening there is a private meeting in the Catholic presbytery in Shepton Mallet to which Pa isn't invited. It is a gathering of the parish "Justice and Peace" committee, which is chaired by Father Carrol, who does exactly what the members order, as he's too weak, confused, and frightened to resist the overwhelming forces of renewal. How can he? For the members of the committee, four middle-aged women, know and have the ear of the Bishop of Clifton, who is very sensitive to even the smallest resistance among his clergy. It's not really a meeting as most of us would understand it, for that would imply a free exchange of ideas and debate. No, the women get together beforehand and work out what amounts to a list of demands which they present to the priest at this gathering on a take-it-or-leave-it basis. They hand Father a copy of an agenda at the top of which is the usual rhetorical question: "How can we best implement the reforms of Vatican II?" Under this is a short list of ideas which the ladies have come up with.

1. Father should appoint a finance committee to oversee all the financial transactions of the parish and supervise the expenditure.
2. Father should publish parish accounts every month and announce at every Sunday Mass how much the collection was for the week.
3. A special area to be allocated to families with children at the back of the church which should be soundproof.
4. All forms of elitism in the Mass should be curtailed, such as anything in Latin.
5. Mr O'Connor and his family should be approached with a view to organising more folk Masses with guitars and recorders supplied by them.
6. The regular Bevan Family choir is too exclusive, and Mr Bevan should invite other members of the parish to sing with them. The music should be simplified to accommodate those who are less proficient at singing.

There is a hush in the room which is interrupted by the clinking of teacups and the sound of false teeth grinding on digestive biscuits as Father Carrol studies the agenda through his half-moon spectacles. Finally, he sits up in his chair and surveys the ladies around the table, one at a time. He takes a deep breath as he sums up all the courage within him.

"I'm sorry, ladies, but this is not the Church I joined. If you insist on these changes then I will submit my resignation to the bishop immediately. I've passed normal retirement age, so he can't refuse." There's an embarrassed silence which is broken by the ringing of the telephone in the hall. The priest leaves the room to answer it and, when he returns, he finds his sitting room empty as his guests have all left. With a sigh he enters the kitchen and picks up the bottle of whisky on the side and slops some into his teacup which he carries back into the sitting room. He switches on the television and settles down to *Coronation Street*. He has just dozed off, having gulped down his whiskey, when the telephone rings again. With difficulty Father Carrol rises from his armchair and makes for the hall. He picks up the receiver and hears the voice of Father Terry Dowding, the bishop's secretary. After some preliminary exchanges, Father Dowding says:

"We've been told that you wish to resign, Father. Is this true?" Carrol is amazed at the speed at which this news has travelled.

"Shall we say, Father, that my parishioners have given me no room for manoeuvre, and I am considering an exit route, yes."

"I'm sorry to hear that, Father," replies Terry. "Perhaps we could meet up and I could help you to reconsider?"

"Well, at the very least I would want to be moved to another parish where my humble talents might be appreciated." After a short pause he adds, "... or perhaps I could retire immediately."

"I'm afraid we've all got to move with the times, now, Father. Lay participation in parish life is the new normal." Father Carrol winces at this. In the good old days, the parish priest was "Pope" in the parish, and he was treated like royalty. The role of lay people was simply to "pray, pay, and obey."

"Can you pop in to see me and the bishop sometime?," says Terry.

"When?"

"How about tomorrow, Father?"

Carrol thinks to himself but doesn't say, "why the almighty hurry?"

SECRET SMOKING AND AN INTERRUPTION

Back at the farm, with lunch over, I, Joe, aged thirteen and number nine from the top, inch my way out of the kitchen hoping not to be spotted by an older sister and presented with a drying up cloth. I emerge from the back door and stride up the garden path to the farm sheds. Keen not to draw attention to myself, I take special care to tease open the green gate as gently as I can and quietly press it shut afterwards. Out of eyesight from the rest of my family, I hurry towards the rabbit hutches and squeeze myself between the low building and the nettles, finally arriving at my den. This hideout is a clearing made from an overgrown hedge, and I have a wide view and early warning of the arrival of any inquisitive brothers and sisters.

With a sigh I pull out an old cigar tin, open it and take out a cigarette, my last one which has been saved for this day.

There are two sides to my young life, which are, firstly, my membership in a large musical family and, secondly, my secret life, which can be more accurately described as my "secret garden." It is this second and furtive life which adds most interest and even excitement to my existence. Most of my secret life involves activities which, although not demonstrably wicked at this stage, are certain to be frowned upon by Ma and Pa, if they thought about it at all, which is doubtful as they have the care of fourteen children, ten of whom are financially dependent on Pa's occupation as the Director of Music at Downside School. The sum total of my illicit activities can be reduced to this: the odd cigarette and the occasional swig out of Pa's gin bottle as I pass the drinks tray. Moments of seclusion, such as this, are gold dust in my life. This is because I am not very popular amongst my brothers and sisters, being rather objectionable and aggressive, so I shun their company as often as I can. In any case I'm usually bored and if I am observed hanging around the farmhouse unoccupied it is inevitable that Ma, who is always frantically busy, will allocate to me some task or other. There are always jobs to do, from sweeping and mopping to repainting the greenhouse, weeding the garden, or cleaning Pa's car. For idle hands there are jobs galore, and knowing this, I prefer to keep out of sight.

As I survey the farm complex from my vantage point, drawing on the sweet smoke, my attention is drawn to the sight of a solitary figure closing the green gate gently, just as I had done, and walking towards me. My younger brother reaches the door to the rabbit hutch and, heaving it open, enters, pulling the door shut behind him. I watch him through a gap in the wooden slats which make up the shed. There are a few rabbits running around and, taking no notice of them, the brother settles down in the corner on a pile of hay and pulls out a Castella cigar, presumably the same one which Pa had complained that he had lost a few days ago and which was a present from Jack, a local farmer. I wait and watch undetected while my brother lights up and breathes in the fumes. They attack my nostrils, and the smell reminds me of Christmas. I resist the temptation to show myself and make common cause with my brother, because the complications which may arise in the future are not to be thought of. I silently wait for the boy to tread out the cigar and quit the rabbit hutch. When all is quiet again, I pop an extra strong mint into my mouth and saunter back to the house and retreat upstairs to my bedroom. Within a few minutes I am lying on my bed listening to my new record of Beethoven's triple concerto.

AN AFTERNOON VISITOR

In the quiet of the afternoon Pa is reading aloud to Ma in the sitting room while she is busy with her pile of mending. Pa is a good reader and puts on different voices for each character of the book. After about half an hour his voice begins to slur and he begins to miss out sentences, eventually lapsing into a contented sleep, his mouth sagging open, and Ma listens to the snores. A game of *Monopoly* is underway in the large kitchen which, as usual, degenerates into a shouting match. At the loud exclamation of "Rent!" Pa wakes up with a jolt and frowns.

"The sooner we ban that game, the better," he mumbles and returns to his dozing. But Ma has also fallen asleep.

Visitors to Parsonage Farm don't knock on the front door, although there's a perfectly good brass door knocker; they just wander in and call out. Ma and Pa are roused by the sound of a car pulling up in the drive and, glancing out of the window, Pa sees Dom Cuthbert emerging from the vehicle.

"It's Cuthers," he announces, and Ma says, "the tea's all ready."

Dom Cuthbert is an elderly and portly monk with thinning grey hair and speaks with a definite lisp. When he sits himself down, he immediately pulls out his silver cigarette holder, twists a cigarette into it, and lights up. As he draws in the smoke his lips give a resounding *smack* and he wheezily inhales. He never seems to exhale the fumes as they are nowhere to be seen. He addresses all his remarks to Pa and, much to her annoyance, hardly acknowledges the presence of Ma. She leaves the room and returns with a plate of thinly sliced homemade bread and butter and a tray of tea. Cuthbert makes an assault on the food as he pops the slices into his mouth, one by one, without talking. Once the bread has been polished off, he slurps his tea and lights another cigarette, *smack!*

"How was your foreign trip, Father?," begins Pa.

"Oh, thuper!" lisps the monk. "I've just spent two weeks at the seminary in Louvain at the request of the abbot to revise my theology."

"Oh?" says Pa, suppressing a yawn.

"Oh yeth. I've learnt such a lot. I'm particularly impressed with the new ideas about us being the people of God."

"What's that?" Pa sits up.

"Well," he continues, "we are saved as the people of God, meaning that it is by our participation in the assembly, regardless of the state of our souls. So, the Church is open to everyone of all faiths, not just Catholics."

"Doesn't sound right to me," interjects Ma.

"We have to stop being so exclusive and we must welcome everybody."

Pa says, "What do you mean by the 'assembly,' Father?"

"I suppose you used to call it the Mass, but that's out of the window now."

"Isn't that what Martin Luther taught?," asked Pa.

"Oh yeth, we've much to learn from Luther!"

"When I go to Mass, I participate by uniting my prayers with those of the celebrant," Ma says. "That's real participation, not just singing hymns and joining in the prayers. I often say my rosary..."

Upon hearing this, Cuthbert bounces up and down crossly in his chair.

"Oh no!" he interrupts. "You have to be more open, that's what the New Mass demands of you. The priest is on the same level as the people now, he's their leader. On the subject of the rosary, the professor at Louvain was very dismissive about repetitive prayer."

"If we abandon our private devotions, Father, how can we participate without our minds wandering to planning what we're going to have for Sunday lunch, especially when we're distracted by the level of noise which you seem to advocate?," asks Ma, mystified.

"Yeth, it's all completely different now. In the New Mass the people of God will have to make an extra special effort, that's what the Holy Spirit asks, rather than being passive onlookers."

"RENT!" comes the shout from the kitchen. "Mayfair, four thousand pounds please." Pa rises from his chair. "I'm going to have to put a stop to that dreadful game," he says. "No, Roger," Ma replies quietly. "Leave them, they're happy."

After Dom Cuthbert departs, Ma and Pa sit back down. Pa sighs. "This is a nightmare, only I don't think we'll ever wake up. Cuthers is only repeating the same stuff which they taught me in Anglican theological college before the war. It looks like I'm back in the Church of England." Ma nods. Pa continues: "Trouble is, it all sounds so, well, positive and well-meaning, I can imagine lots of clergy being seduced by it. But it's pure poison, nonetheless."

A DIFFICULT MEETING

The next morning, Father Carrol parks his Fiat in the gravelled drive outside the main diocesan offices in Bristol. With difficulty he emerges from the vehicle and walks up the stone steps to the front and arrives red-faced and panting in the reception. By a notice on the desk saying "please ring bell for attention" there is a handbell, which he rings. Carrol sits down in a slightly frayed leather chair and glances at the pictures on the wall. There is the Sacred Heart, there is the old photograph of a smiling St Theresa, and, finally, with pride of place, a large colour photograph of the current bishop, Jim. He is standing in his nylon rainbow-coloured vestments and holding a wooden crozier topped by a bent crucifix. Carrol notices something strange about the bishop's chasuble so, rising from his chair to get a closer look, he sees that it is decorated with the emblem of the Campaign for Nuclear Disarmament. Surrounding the laughing bishop is a group of African children, also laughing. Carrol cringes. Footsteps in the distance echo in a passage and eventually approach the reception area—not the clump of black shoes, but more the squeak of sports shoes. The door is pushed open and in walks Father Dowding in a tracksuit.

"Oh, Hi Father!," he says breathlessly. After a few minutes of friendly chat Father Dowding says, "His Lordship has had to go out and has asked me to talk to you myself and has given me full permission to take whatever action I deem necessary in your case, Father."

"A cup of coffee would be nice," replies Carrol.

"Oh, no time for that, I'm afraid. I have to rush off in a moment to chair a meeting of 'Women for Change.'" As far as he is concerned, Carrol thinks, he might as well have said, "Nazis for Euthanasia."

Dowding shows no sign of inviting Carrol into the administration building and places himself in the other leather chair, facing Carrol.

"His Lordship regretfully accepts your offer of resignation, Father."

Carrol sits up with a start.

"Wha...what?"

"Oh yes, you see, you're past retirement age and we can offer you the full retirement package. Can you be out of the presbytery in seven days?"

"It doesn't sound like you're giving me any choice."

"Well, no, not really. Where will you go?"

"To my sister in Northampton, I expect."

"That's lucky," answers Dowding. "We have good contacts in that diocese and can fix you up with some part-time work."

"I'm sorry to say this, Father," says Carrol. "But once I'm out, I'm really out. I have no wish to say this New Mass ever again. It would drive me bonkers."

"Yes, I can understand that. You see, with the New Mass you only get out of it what you are prepared to put in. In the old days you were able to mumble through the Latin Mass without so much as thinking about what you were doing."

"I can't understand why a priest as young as you can make such assumptions about other priests' intentions as they say Mass. You sound very arrogant to me. By the way, who's taking over at my parish?"

"We have one of our best young priests going there to reverse the decline. He's what we would call 'dynamic.'"

Carrol is furious. "Decline? What decline?" He is shouting now. "It was only when we imposed the New Mass last year that people started to stay away, and who can blame them?"

Dowding attempted to speak but Carrol waved him silent.

"And while we're about it," he continued, "you have been encouraging rebellion in my parish. I've been forced to set up committees for everything and they are always peopled by the same female agitators. My authority has almost evaporated. I also find it very insulting that the bishop decided not to meet me himself. We were at the English College together."

"That's progress for you, Father!"

Carrol replied angrily. "Well, I won't give a fig for your chances. You will empty the churches as sure as eggs is eggs. After all the experiments have run their course, you'll discover that the people want the truth, not gimmicks."

"Well let's agree to disagree, Father?"

"Tell you what," answers Carrol. "Let's just disagree and leave it at that!"

Returning to his car, Father Carrol mumbles to himself. "Jumped-up little whatsit!"

CHAPTER 5

Turning the Screw

1972: A LITURGICAL CONSPIRACY

On a Friday during the winter term, at a quarter to nine in the morning, the little green van, registration number VLX 444, arrives in the quadrangle of Downside School as usual. It is driven by Pa and, next to him in the passenger seat, is Rupert who is the eldest of the three Bevan boys attending the school as dayboys. In the back of the van, and balancing awkwardly on leather cushions, are me and Jeremy. Pa has held the post of Director of Music at the school since 1956, a year before I was born and two years before Jeremy's arrival. As we emerge out of the back door of the vehicle we are assailed by, firstly, the cacophony of electronic rock music blaring out of an assortment of open windows, and, secondly, by shouts of "rabbit! rabbit!" which echo across the tarmac. This taunt is caused not only by the knowledge that the Bevan Family consists of fourteen children, but also by the fact that they are disliked intensely for their aloofness and superiority. Pa locks the van and enters the doors of the main school building. He crosses the main hall which is bustling with boys in their black jackets and grey pinstripe trousers, all clutching books and papers as they find their classrooms. He gets whiffs of body odour and stale cigarettes as he climbs up eight flights of stairs to his own room at the top of Roberts' Tower. It is only a small room, home to an upright black piano with a fitted pedal board, two army surplus green cupboards, and four desks.

Pa settles down in his room in Roberts' Tower at Downside to mark an essay and fingers his pipe, reaching for his tin of *Three Nuns*. His peace is interrupted by the jangling of the internal telephone on the windowsill. He stands up, walks over, and picks up the receiver. He listens to the voice on the other end and then says, "certainly, headmaster, I'll be with you in ten minutes." Before he leaves, however, Pa makes a quick telephone call to Dom Cuthbert McCann, his closest friend by far and a valuable one at that, for it is Dom Cuthbert who has his ear to the ground and is able to give Pa advance warning of any future conspiracies being hatched in the nearby monastery. Pa has noticed that, during the last twelve months at least, plot after plot has been hatched amongst monastic circles to try to undermine his position as master of the liturgical music in the abbey church. Fortunately, these schemes have come to nothing thanks to some deft footwork. Pa, having received the appropriate intelligence from his friend, replaces the receiver and experiences that usual sinking feeling. Dom Cuthbert has told him about an "initiative" (the latest buzzword) concerning the music at the school Mass, only this time it is in collaboration with some of the senior boys in the school. "Here we go," he groans, "another case of Bevan *contra mundum.*" He settles back into his chair and lights his pipe. "I'll make them wait a bit longer," he thinks, as he inhales a wad of thick smoke.

Four flights of stairs down from Pa's room is a long corridor full of classrooms. Lessons have been suspended this week because the whole school is on annual retreat, giving the schoolmasters a welcome opportunity to catch up on paperwork and sit around in the staff common room smoking and gossiping. The first classroom, number 5, is nonetheless full of teenage boys who are watching a black and white film about the life of St Francis of Assisi. Almost no one is paying attention to the screen and there is no supervision. Someone has relieved Watkinson of his black shoe, and an impromptu game of touch rugby develops. Boys are jumping across desks and yelling at the tops of their voices. Nobody in authority knows or cares what is going on. The ancient film projector is knocked onto the floor and the film ceases, but the shoe is tossed up into the air again and again to the whoops and cries of the assembled company. Suddenly the school bell rings, and they all pile out into the corridor to make their escape, leaving Watkinson behind to hunt for his shoe.

A JESUIT RETREAT

In another part of the school Father "call me Eddie" Peach is taking a class of about twenty boys and the theme of the lesson is "Who am I?" Peach is a young priest who is very earnest as he delivers the lesson in his northern vowels. He is dressed in workmanlike clothes beloved of the members of the modern Jesuit clergy—a short-sleeved open-necked red shirt with black slacks, complete with gym shoes on his feet. If one met him in the street one could make an educated guess that Peach had some connection with religion, but that's about it as he displays no visible sign that he's a priest unless, of course, you count the silver cross appended to his key ring which he fiddles with as he talks. On the desk at which he is sitting is a Phillips mini cassette player.

"Ah think Simon and Garfunkel really sum it up in their song, which Ah'll now play for yer. Feel free to sing along if you're in the mood," he quips with a smirk. With that he depresses the "play" button on the cassette machine and the room is filled with a blaring rendition of "Bridge Over Troubled Water." The boys loll around and adopt postures of boredom, but they sit up straight as they see Father Peach pulling out a packet of Benson and Hedges special filters. As he lights one and breathes in the smoke, Wilson calls out to him, "er... may we smoke, please Father?"

"Call me 'Eddie' and, yes, of course you may smoke."

Immediately the whole room transforms into a hive of activity as various boys reach into the inner recesses of their clothes for cigarettes, cigars, and rolling tobacco. Eventually the room fills with a choking fug and Father Peach opens the windows. I am sitting in the back row and reach for my cigar tin from which I fish out a Number Six. Hughes is lighting a pipe.

Someone puts a hand up: "Please can I have a cigarette... Eddie?," he asks hesitantly.

Without answering, Father Peach hands over his entire box of cigarettes to the boy, which is passed round, and is finally returned to the priest empty of its contents. Peach examines the packet and pulls a face. The music fades out and he continues his talk.

"...and you can see that Mary Magdalen really looves Jesus and is quite oopset when he doesn't return that love." The tape machine is activated once more, "...and I've haa'd so-o many me-en before, and in many, many wa-ays... he's just one more." The music of *Jesus Christ Superstar* rises and falls over the heads of somnolent pupils who contentedly draw and suck in their life-giving nicotine. I start to think to myself that, if this is the new religion everyone seems to object to, it is actually very exciting.

BEVAN *CONTRA MUNDUM*

Pa makes his way thoughtfully across the school hall, past the junior house day room and the Sligger history library to the Old House. As he enters, he leaves the noises and smells of school behind him and finds himself in a world of fitted carpets, clicking typewriters and buzzing telephones, where people speak in whispers. Arriving at a door marked "Headmaster" which has traffic lights fastened to the door frame—green for "enter" and red for "wait"—he knocks. The green light is signalled, and Pa enters the well-appointed, not to say luxurious, suite of Dom Raphael, the headmaster. There are four people sitting in a semicircle facing the large desk, behind which sits Dom Raphael, relaxed and cheerful. His black scapular is tossed over his right shoulder, workmanlike, revealing his black tunic and a row of silver pens emerging out of his breast pocket. Those sitting around are the art master John Crocket ("what's this got to do with him?," Pa asks himself), Dom Ambrose, a senior housemaster and an historically active revolutionary in all things religious, and, finally, two senior school prefects with long dirty hair. Observing the two boys, Pa is overcome with a sense of dread. He is outnumbered and it is just as he foretold, Bevan *contra mundum*.

Pa sits in an empty chair which has been reserved for him next to the two schoolboys and faces the headmaster across the desk. Dom Raphael opens the meeting by welcoming everyone and finally gets to the point.

"Max," he says, turning to the boy with the longest and dirtiest hair, the dandruff settling on his shoulders like the first snow. "Would you like to open the bowling?"

Max clears his throat and starts speaking in the familiar Downside drawl.

"Well, we've had a meeting amongst us sixth formers an' we fink that Sunday Mass is, frankly, rather boring 'cos there's no participation by those present. It's like a concert with us as spectators. Also, the music which the choir sings is elitist..."

Upon hearing this, Pa harrumphs and behaves like a jumping bean in front of the fire. Dom Raphael holds up his hand and cautions the director of music to silence.

"I mean," continues Max, "the Mass should reflect our everyday lives and loves an' that." Dom Ambrose nods briskly at this as does the other senior boy. John Crocket sits cross-legged, stroking his beard thoughtfully. Pa's blood pressure rises.

"What nonsense...!" But he is again silenced by the headmaster.

Crocket speaks, "I wonder if it would be better if we could make our points uninterrupted?"

"Hear, hear!" says Dom Ambrose.

"I mean, classical music at Mass is okay if you like that stuff but, anyway, if you're sitting halfway down the church, you can't hear anything apart from a jumble of sound." Max is getting into his stride. "The Mass used to be a paternalistic 'we know what's best for you' kind of thing, but we've grown up now, thanks to Vatican II, and we should really make some changes."

"This is intolerable!"

Pa receives a warning look from Dom Raphael.

"Cyprian," says Raphael, addressing the other vagrant-like boy, "what have you to say?"

"Err...well...what we want is an experimental Mass where me and my friends would put on a dynamic liturgy involving the participation of most of the school. It would be relevant and meaningful."

Pa explodes.

"I can't believe I'm hearing this!" he bellows, causing those around him to start.

"Roger," interjects Dom Raphael, grimly but gently. "Please calm down, we'll come to you soon. Dom Ambrose, what is your view?"

Ambrose, a tall young monk with ginger hair, answers, "yes, thank you, headmaster. Now that Clifton diocese has designated Downside as a centre for liturgical experiment, I think Cyprian's ideas are very apt. It's high time we caught up with the dynamism which is operating in the Church as a whole."

"What utter nonsense!"

"Roger," says Dom Raphael with a knowing smile, "please give us your opinion now. As director of music in the abbey, would you be happy to hand over the running of the music to the boys from time to time?"

"No, I would object most strongly to this. It sounds like reducing the Mass to the level of a kiddie's playtime. God requires the very best which we can offer, and that means singing the music written specially for worship. The hard work which my choir puts in to produce high quality music on Sundays can only be a good thing."

Ambrose shakes his head, "But Roger," he replies, "the music you sing at the moment was written for the old Latin Mass. We've moved on, surely, and for the New Mass we need new music, don't we?"

Dom Raphael interjects. "Also, you're forgetting that much of the music you sing is in English, such as anthems, which were never sung during the Latin Mass, were they?"

Crocket indicates that he wishes to speak. "Yes, John?" says Raphael.

"We have to do something about the music in the abbey before boys start taking matters into their own hands. They're bored rigid on Sundays, and many are agitating for separate Masses in their individual houses instead of the school Mass." Roger thinks to himself, but doesn't say, "Was that a threat of some kind?"

"Yes, absolutely," says Raphael. "Roger, I hope you don't mind but on Sunday week I'm prepared to allow the boys to do their own thing and arrange a Mass in accordance with current thinking. Dom Ambrose, I'll give you overall command of everything to make sure that the results are, shall we say, sensible."

WANDERING THROUGH DOWNSIDE

Pa, outgunned and outnumbered, shrugs his shoulders and after making a cursory nod to those present, leaves the room to return to Roberts Tower. It is the half-hour mid-morning break between retreat sessons and as he walks through the main hall, he notices a group of school prefects, in their white waistcoats and flowing silk handkerchiefs, lounging against the windowsill. They are miserable and pull exaggeratedly long faces because they have just lost heavily at rugger. It is noticeable that these overdressed dandies are failing in their obligations to maintain order in the school to the extent that junior masters have to supervise daily activities, such as taking prep in the Gasquet Hall and lunch queues.

At lunchtime, Gasquet Hall, the main classroom where all the boys without rooms of their own do their prep, is echoing to the sound of the school television bolted to the wall high up at the front. A handful of boys are sitting around watching *Crown Court*. Dom Hilary Steuart enters the room and switches off the television, reminding those present that they are on school retreat. The boys sullenly and resentfully leave the room.

As the boys wander through the main hall towards their dining rooms, Dom Cuthbert, sitting on a bench as usual, calls out as they pass, "hello Thimon, hello Crithpin, hello Juthtin!"

Lunch in the main refectory is served to the boys who queue up holding chipped wooden trays and macaroni cheese is slopped onto their plates, which they carry to a table. The room is always full, and the long tables crowded with diners, all except one long table at the end of which the three female pupils, the first ever at the school, dine in the distance. They sit alone and the rest of the long table is empty of boys so my brother Rupert takes pity on them and sits down next to them to chat and eat his lunch.

Returning from the main dining room and going down the steps to arrive in the main hall, to the left are the main school lavatories, known as the "yard." Entering this place, one sees rows of urinals and then, as far as the eye can observe, a long passage bordered by numberless cubicles, many with their locks broken. At the far end of the passage a few boys meet to enjoy a post-lunch cigarette uninterrupted by the authorities, who won't go near the place. Veterans of this pastime for the rest of their lives, no doubt, will associate the smell of cigarettes with the smell of urine, and, presumably, vice versa.

1974: DOM CUTHBERT TELLS A STORY

It is Advent, three weeks before Christmas. The huge fireplace in the sitting room at Parsonage Farm is belching woodsmoke, and it is difficult to keep one's eyes open. This is why most of the Bevan children smell pleasingly smoky during the months of autumn and winter. Pa opens all the windows, letting in the cold, which rather defeats the object of having a fire. The smoke does vanish as the chimney heats up and soon the windows are shut, and the occupants of the room begin to warm up. Later that Sunday afternoon, Dom Cuthbert graces the family with another visit, and having consumed a plate of bread and butter, has a strange tale to recount. He can barely contain his amusement.

"Last Sunday evening, I was sitting in the armchair in my bedroom at the Great Western Hotel in Paddington, which was on the fourth floor of the building, looking forward to going down to the bar, when I noticed a strange smell. 'I know that smell,' I thought to myself, and suddenly I heard the sound of a handbell tinkling. As this noise and smell seem to be coming from the carpeted passage outside my room, I opened my bedroom door and peered out into the corridor. At first, I saw nothing, but suddenly there emerged from a hotel room on my right a man wearing a black cassock and a white cotta who was swinging a smoking thurible. Behind him I saw two men, similarly dressed, holding brass candlesticks. At the end of the procession was a priest wearing red and gold vestments and a black biretta on his head. In his hands he held a veiled chalice." Cuthbert chuckled.

"The procession went past me and disappeared into another room a bit further down the passage. At first, I thought I was witnessing something from the paranormal, but I ventured out of my room and tiptoed to the door through which the procession had disappeared. I could hear the crying of babies, and then a little choir struck up with 'Asperges me,' which I haven't heard sung anywhere for many years. A little later I inquired at the hotel reception as to the meaning of this spectacle and she told me that a group called the Society of St Pius X booked two rooms every Sunday. She wanted to know if they disturbed me, and I replied in the negative."

Ma and Pa listen attentively to the story but neither make any comments, and this for two reasons. Firstly, both parents are at loggerheads about the crisis in the Catholic Church, Pa being grudgingly accepting of the reforms which Ma strongly detests. Secondly, there's no point in discussing any of this with Cuthbert who, when it comes to Vatican II, is a firebrand in its defence.

BUMPING ALONG THE BOTTOM

In common with so many Catholic families at this time, religion is fast becoming a banned subject because of the high emotions felt by many in the Bevan family. One of the most outspoken critics of the new liturgy is me, as I have undertaken to read up what Pa terms "poisonous literature," a monthly periodical called *Approaches*, written by Hamish Fraser using a home printer and photocopied multiple times. In this crudely produced publication, covered in ink smudges, Fraser opens my eyes to the fact that, contrary to the confidence trick practised on the Catholic laity, the Church not so long ago was holy, peaceful, and normal. He describes the goings-on at a strange seminary in Switzerland where young seminarians are taught "the old stuff" and learn to say the old Latin Mass exclusively. Also, Fraser goes into great detail about the shocking persecution of the archbishop who runs the institution. I am amazed by the treachery and subterfuge practiced by a gang of mainly French bishops in their attempts to stamp out the seminary.

As the Bevan children prepare for Christmas, the family choir rehearsals become more intense and time-consuming. There is the normal run of Christmas concerts and carol services. Also, Pa has decided that the time has come to make a record. Two days have been set aside for this purpose next week as a recording engineer will arrive to organise it. Although it is the holidays, the family choir doesn't sing at Mass any longer as it was dismissed by the new parish priest at Shepton Mallet. Pa still plays the organ there but only to accompany the boring congregational Masses so beloved of the reformers. Mass at Shepton Mallet is a trial and everyone in the family hates it.

The new priest, Father Meehan, a jolly rotund man with a large shiny face and round spectacles, is a master of the unexpected. Rather than keep to the stated format of the Mass as set down in the annoying sheets of paper which everybody holds, he digresses into a homemade liturgy and calls upon contributions from the reluctant and embarrassed congregation, greatly diminished in numbers nowadays. The result of this is that the Sunday Mass, which used to be attended by all the Catholic families in the parish, is gradually abandoned by them as they either give up religion completely, go to a more bearable event in a nearby parish, or even go to a shortened anticipatory Mass on Saturday evening which, preposterously, has now been allowed by the authorities. Father Meehan has adopted the habit of encouraging "spontaneous" displays of affection at the "kiss of peace" which happens just before the *Agnus Dei*, as he strolls down the altar steps and mingles with the people, laughing, kissing, hugging, and shaking hands with everyone—except for the Bevans, of course, whom he studiously avoids. As he returns to the altar, he turns his head around to the people behind him and announces casually, "Lamb of God..." and the people take up the prayer.

(Short digression: my uncle Rupert, who was my mother's elder brother, related to me the following incident in his local Catholic parish. "I had a friend who had stopped going to church a few years ago and, after much persuasion, finally agreed to accompany me to Mass the next day, which was a Sunday. As it was a folk Mass with a lot of congregational participation, my friend was visibly unimpressed and said that he had simply been reminded of the reason he had lapsed in the first place. The following Sunday I went to Mass again—only this time my friend decided that he couldn't face it. After Mass I had the following conversation with the parish priest: 'I see you didn't bring your friend today, why was that?' 'Oh, Father, it's just that he objected to the handshaking.' 'Is that all? Tell him that if he comes again, I'll give him a big hug!'")

What is even more irritating is Meehan's preference for the young children of the parish, whom he calls up to the altar to be interviewed by him.

One of these poor kids has a very strange and carrying voice and Father leaves him till last and, when the boy's voice cackles over the loudspeakers, everyone laughs, as the priest intended. Meehan often likes the children to stand in a circle round the altar whilst he recites the Eucharistic Prayer. It is during one of these episodes that I, my mind still full of anger at the treatment of Archbishop Lefebvre, solemnly rise from my pew and, with all the eyes of the congregation upon me, march out of the church, taking care to give the door a good slam. The revolution in the Catholic Church has spawned a generation of "door-slammers." My first encounter with this phenomenon was when Mrs Todd noisily departed during Mass after our family choir had struck up with the four-part Mass by William Byrd. It is with this woman very much in mind that I do the same thing in response to the high jinks at the altar. Several years later, and before we rediscover the Old Mass, my wife and I become seasoned "door-slammers," especially in France, where the provocations during Mass can be unendurable.

CHAPTER 6

My Apostasy

1976: *NISI DOMINUS AEDIFICAVERIT DOMUM, IN VANUM LABORAVERUNT QUI AEDIFICANT EAM.*[1]

In the hot and extremely dry summer of this year we welcome the television cameras into our lives. They are filming a documentary called *Harmony at Parsonage Farm*. Anyone can see this film for themselves as it is on YouTube. In *Two Families* I give an overall account of the activities of the film crew, but there are a few other matters which I now call to mind for further clarification.

I very much gain the impression that our parents are slightly uneasy and seem to be apologetic for the lives which they are leading. Pa, for example, seems to be yearning for a life of ease and leisure as opposed to his current existence, fraught as it is with inconveniences and money troubles: "If I was able to retire and live a life of idleness," he says, "then I would live a life of idleness." Ma, in her own way, seems to be saying things on the lines of: "I hope I have passed on to my children an interest and curiosity in the things of life." She also appears

---

[1] "Unless the Lord build the house, they labour in vain that build it" (Psalm 126:1).

to be reticent about having had so many children: "I love children and accept them from God." The implication being that large families are no longer a duty but a mere preference. I can imagine the average viewer shouting at the screen: "Why couldn't you use contraception?" Many of the children who are interviewed (you can see it for yourself) seem to distance themselves from the family and like to portray themselves as loners. There seems to be little appetite for proclaiming, as Catholics should, that large happy and devout families are the building blocks of the Church and of society as a whole.

The most important task of Catholic parents is to hand on the Faith to their offspring and this is not mentioned in the film. Indeed, one sibling states openly that the unifying force in our family is "music...and our parents' faith." No mention here of the *children's* faith at all. In fact, during the whole programme, where all sorts of opinions get an airing, religion of any sort barely gets a mention. There are no shots of the family worshipping, save for singing a motet in the Anglican church in Croscombe, which is stage-managed for the cameras and never happened as a real event. To be fair, Ma does state that her ultimate objective is to get to heaven, but she neglects to mention that she is striving to achieve the same for her children. However, as I never tire of reminding my readers, this is not really the fault of my parents, as the state of the family in 1976 represents a microcosm of the crisis in the Catholic Church worldwide. If Pa were still alive, I can imagine him reading this paragraph and exclaiming: "Why do you keep on bringing religion into everything?" It is this attitude which encapsulates the growing secularism amongst Catholics after the Second Vatican Council.

1982: FURTHER EDUCATION

What can I say about Bristol Polytechnic, now renamed the University of the West of England? "That great bus-seat of learning," remarks Pa, caustically. I am studying for a law degree and in my final year. Mainly constructed of concrete and glass, a sprawling pile of prefabricated buildings designed in a style very familiar in communist countries, the polytechnic site is perched on a hill, surrounded by a network of motorways and rundown industrial parks. Half of the college has not been built yet, and so I have got used to the ubiquitous presence of builders and cranes. The nearest town, on the edge of the urban sprawl of Bristol, is Filton, famous only for housing the headquarters of Rolls Royce. To be honest, I hate studying law. My poor brain is not able to absorb massive amounts of useless and detailed information and spew it out at examinations. Although I eventually graduate by the skin of my teeth with a B.A (Hons) Third Class, I afterwards find that a general knowledge of how the legal system works helps me because it is useful to know what a mortgage is, or how parliament works, for example. Ma used to say that a study of law ensured, at least, that "one knew one's onions."

I encounter the usual problem of being unable to make friends, having my nose permanently in the air. I am universally disliked for the simple reason that I distance myself from my fellow students, most of whom I consider to be *oiks*.[2] There is some justification for my reaction to my classmates as I discover that the "pop culture" has a firm grip on the whole student population. Everyone dresses in T-shirts, flared jeans, and desert boots. These T-shirts are emblazoned with various outrageous slogans and pictures of Che Guevara or other student heroes. Drugs are just coming in and one can always spot the partakers of cannabis a mile away. They have this glassy-eyed and unblinking staring look. Against my better judgment, I attend a party in a student residence and in the corner of the front room sit a few partygoers giggling manically—these are the druggies. One particular third-year chap arrives at our Administrative Law seminar positively stoned. On Friday and Saturday evenings I have to lock myself in my room as many students are either stoned, or hopelessly drunk, or both. On these nights I am kept awake by the sounds of drunken shouts and smashing glass. On the following Sunday morning the whole campus is eerily silent.

I notice how people who listen habitually to pop music cannot keep still and when they're not actually listening, jig up and down while mouthing silently the words to some song or other. This is very off-putting and makes one doubt their sanity as they seem to be completely self-absorbed. My own love of classical music, particularly the works of Bach, Beethoven, and Brahms, is a complete mystery to my fellow students and marks me out as an oddball. It is almost as though I am living in

---

[2] An "oik" is a rude and unpleasant man from a low social class.

a foreign country, finding it impossible to discover the language of the inhabitants, thus enhancing my sense of isolation. I have always been used to conversation in my own family, usually quick-fire repartee, of a certain intellectual level and covering a wide range of subjects. And yet, here at Bristol, I am unable to converse with my fellow students unless I have mastered such topics as: what was on the television last night, my drunken antics the previous evening, or the scripts of *Monty Python's Flying Circus*, which many people are able to trot out faultlessly and verbatim.

Many of the male students in my year have paired off with the females and I am aware of the results of sexual immorality in this way: a male and female student go through a kind of process which starts when they make friends. So far all is well, and they will be very jolly together, often regarded as the life and soul of any gathering. "Steve and Tess are so happy together!" their friends remark. When Steve and Tess consummate their relationship, they become emotionally dependent upon each other. Finally, they move into the same flat and share a bed. Things are now on the slide, and they run out of conversation, sitting together mute at parties. Such is their emotional dependency that if Steve, for example, even speaks to another woman, Tess reacts with jealous accusations. The inevitable and hurtful bust-up soon follows. We have all noticed mute couples at gatherings who just sit there and hold hands. How wise are the teachings of the Catholic Church which demand chaste abstinence until after the ring is on the finger!

It is all very well for me to go on about chastity before marriage, because in actual fact, whilst I am studying in Bristol, I have lost all interest in my religion, and I would gladly accept an offer from any female student. But as it is, most of the girls dislike me so the opportunity never comes my way. Perish the thought that I should make a virtue of a necessity!

At the beginning of the academic year, I am voted in as treasurer to the fencing club, and this requires me to collect the subscriptions and organise the annual club disco. For some reason, the other members do not want a disco, which is funded by the students' union, and decide, rather, that we should all go out to a cheap restaurant. I make an appointment with the union treasurer and state our desire, asking whether the union would fund this event wholly or, at least, in part. The answer is a flat "no." He insists that it is a disco or nothing.

Having mentioned already that my interest in being a devout Catholic has more or less melted away, I do maintain a connection with a few of the students at my college who are members of the Catholic Union of Students. This is because, paradoxically, I still want to be regarded as a Catholic despite my practical apostasy. Sitting down to lunch one day in the college canteen I am joined by another student who still goes to Mass and he, like me, is alert to the widespread liturgical abuses. He tells me that at a Mass recently in the Bristol University chaplaincy, during the "bidding prayers"[3] the celebrant invited contributions "from the floor" and this exchange took place:

---

3 That is, the Prayer of the Faithful or General Intercessions.

My Apostasy

PRIEST: "Lord, hear us."

CONGREGATION: "Lord graciously hear us."

PRIEST: "Would anyone else like to suggest their own petitions?"

STUDENT: "Let us always be mindful that Jesus Christ was an ordinary bloke like us!"

PRIEST: "Lord, hear us."

CONGREGATION: "Lord graciously hear us."

ANOTHER STUDENT: "Hang on! I don't agree with that! Let us be mindful that Jesus Christ was the Son of God!"

PRIEST: "Lord, hear us."

CONGREGATION: "Lord graciously hear us."

CLIFTON CATHEDRAL CHOIR

My other new activity is joining the choir of Clifton cathedral as a bass. I am not particularly interested in the religious aspect but prefer to do something more constructive on my Sunday mornings than stay in bed nursing a hangover. If there is a single adjective which sums up this cathedral and its services, it is "bleak." The building, which wouldn't look out of place on our college campus, is also made of concrete and glass, reminding me somehow of a crashed aeroplane. The interior of the building is like an aircraft hangar with a central altar surrounded by seats. The choir is jolly good, however, and we sing a wide variety of music, some of which is composed by "Catholic" musicians and verges on the experimental. I do notice, though, how the music we sing is not really liturgical and while we perform, for example, Mozart's "Ave Verum," nothing is going on at the altar. The celebrant and the servers merely sit down, waiting for us to finish. One particular priest cannot resist checking his watch from his comfy chair. There is a lot of *Missa de Angelis* and Credo III, which represent a nodding concession to the conservative elements in the congregation. Our choir Mass is at 11.30 on Sunday morning and before that there is a "family Mass" with the ubiquitous guitars and recorders. As I arrive at the cathedral I see hordes of people, and many children, leaving the building having participated in "Lord of the Dance" and other chestnuts. In spite of the fact that I haven't been to confession for many years, I receive communion along with everyone else. I feel I have to, because if I remained in my place instead of going up to the altar steps, I would stick out like a sore thumb.

In May we are looking forward to the UK visit of Pope John Paul II, and especially the open-air Mass at Coventry, where the Clifton cathedral choir is to have pride of place. As the Mass will take place on Pentecost Sunday we have to learn a long-drawn-out mantra, "Veni Sancte Spiritus," composed by some "go to" composer and which is almost hypnotic in its dreariness. On and on it goes, verse after verse, with small variations. On the Sunday morning in question, we sing the same phrases over and over again quietly, whilst sometimes a tenor soloist trills over the top, or a microphone-hogging female adds her own contribution. The result can only be described as toe-curlingly awful! The choir is supposed to be joined in their repeated mantra by the 80,000 faithful present at the airfield but, as far as I can hear, few of them bother to sing. The readings from the microphone are accompanied by teenage girls at the altar steps, wearing leotards and prancing around slowly. (I am not inventing this, as it can all be seen on YouTube!) I quietly confirm to myself that I shall never return to the Catholic Church, ever! His Holiness preaches a long sermon about "peace." This does not go down too well as the Falklands War is nearing its conclusion, with the UK indulging in a period of nationalistic jingoism encouraged by the Prime Minister, Margaret Thatcher.

1983: CLERK IN A LAW FIRM

In my quest to be a great lawyer I am working as an articled clerk for Messrs. Macdonald, Ramsey and Company, of Frith Street, Soho, London. This is a firm of solicitors which specialises in the worst areas of criminal law, and petty crime constitutes its daily fare. We are what is known as a "legal aid factory" which handles literally dozens of cases on a daily basis. Most of the sad individuals, whom we refer to as "clients," are charged with pickpocketing, possession of cannabis, and "soliciting." Soliciting is a boom industry in the environs of Soho, where prostitutes are arrested merely for approaching potential (usually willing) customers in the shop doorways.

On my first working day at the law firm, having just graduated, I make sure that I arrive punctually at the offices of Macdonald, Ramsey & Co. before nine o'clock in the morning, so as to create a good impression. I enter the front door and ascend the stairs to the first floor, where their offices are situated. The door to the solicitor's office is locked and there's no sign of life. I sit on the top stair until ten-thirty when, at last, steps approach from below. I am greeted by a young man in a shabby raincoat, clearly hung over, as he examines me wearily and produces a bunch of keys.

"Who is it you want to see?," he asks quizzically.

"I'm the new articled clerk and I'm starting today."

"First I've heard of it," he answers with a shrug.

The interior of the offices is a reminder of those of Mr Micawber, as described by Charles Dickens in *David Copperfield*. They never seem to gain the attentions of a cleaner and there is an overpowering smell of stale food. Above all, they are unheated, and the staff have to wear their overcoats when it is cold.

The management of the firm is in the hands of the senior partner, who has a temperament which can only be described as volcanic. The difficulty which we staff have with this neatly turned-out gentleman is that one never knows where one stands with him. When he returns to the office after a liquid lunch, we find him relaxed and at his very best, agreeing to all our requests with a benevolent twinkle in his eye. The main problem is that we hardly ever see him and, if he is present in his magnificently decorated office, we have to ascertain what kind of mood he is in. If things are not going well for some reason, our senior partner will be found in a towering rage, shouting at everyone upon the flimsiest of excuses, and even angrily destroying items in his office. We then end up cowering in our little rooms with the doors firmly shut in order to avoid his attentions. This solicitor also has long alcohol-fuelled shouting matches with the other partner of the firm and this at least takes the pressure off the rest of us. It may be that the arguments arise out of the lengthy and unexplained absences of the senior partner.

The daily activities of the firm consist, amongst other things, in taking statements from clients, many of whom are vagrants and some often hopelessly drunk. Also, the switchboard, a primitive affair with plugs which have to be inserted into correct slots, is constantly ringing as court deadlines come and go. Barristers often ring up from court, angrily asking "Where the hell is everybody?" Some of our clients are banned by the magistrates' court from entering the West End of London as a condition of their bail. From time to time, we are telephoned by West End Central police station saying they have such a person in custody, and the client has explained to the police that the only reason why he's in the vicinity is because he's on his way to visit us, his solicitors. I am manning the switchboard one day when I answer such a call from the police: "We are detaining Mr Jones, who was wandering around the West End. He says he's on his way to see you. Can you confirm that you're expecting him?" I check the office diary and reply that we are not expecting him. There is hell to pay for this from the other staff here as I am expected to lie.

I spend many days hanging around crown court buildings waiting for our cases to come on. I am sick of weak coffee and lengthy conferences with our clients in the holding cells. Many times, there is confusion with the transport which ferries the defendants from prison to court and whole days are wasted whilst we hunt for our client who has not arrived. Witnesses for the defence often disappear, leaving our case in a state of collapse and our barrister having to explain to the cross judge what has happened, and would he agree to an adjournment? The answer is often in the negative. Many of the barristers whom we instruct have only received the brief the night before or turn up with no idea of what the case is about. If a case actually goes to trial, the incompetence of some of the members of the bar is quite embarrassing. A common error made by young barristers is to muddle up the names of witnesses. Here is a typical example of this:

BARRISTER: "What is your opinion of Mr Jones?"
WITNESS: "I *am* Mr Jones!"

I fail to understand why a whole crown court trial is organised, lasting for perhaps two days, because our chap has been in possession of enough cannabis to fit into a small matchbox. The cost to the taxpayer is massive and the whole situation is becoming increasingly hopeless. With so many cases on the go, my firm just plays the system. We never advise someone to plead guilty in the magistrates' court if it is possible to have the case transferred to the crown court simply because we can then get a higher fee scale.

Because our firm is located in Soho, we're the last port of call for many Chinese immigrants who have exhausted all the processes which might delay, or prevent, their deportation. My instructions from above are to smile, give them some hope, and take a full statement. Above all, I am told to take an advance of fees, which they readily hand over in grubby ten-pound notes. Having received the money we all know that their situation is quite hopeless, and we won't see them again. And this is what transpires, with the firm pocketing perhaps £200 for nothing.

Some of our criminal clients seek advice about their possible "civil" claims. Usually these are directed against the police who, so they say, beat them up. Also, there are claims against hospitals, previous employers, and just about anybody else they can think of. As we smell money, we gladly take these on because the legal aid fund will pay for everything, within reason, right up to an appeal to the House of Lords.

If there is one overriding feature of the legal profession, it is that everybody lies. Our clients lie all the time to us. I know this because a cursory reading of their statements shows up obvious inconsistencies and contradictions. The police lie, often recklessly, in order to secure the convictions upon which their career advancement depends. One of our regular clients, a woman who keeps on getting arrested for prostitution, having pleaded guilty, theatrically and convincingly weeps in the witness box. She is so good at it that she melts the heart of the judge and gets off with a minimum penalty.

One afternoon I am instructed to deliver a court document to one of our "ladies of the night" who operates out of the *Golden Girl Club*, just around the corner from our office in Soho. Opposite a handmade shoe shop I find the seedy club and enter through the front door, which is ajar. I find myself in a tatty bar area with a makeshift stage in one corner. I call out for assistance but nobody's about, so I walk up to the bar, which is littered with dirty glasses and overflowing ashtrays, and observe what appears to be a bar tariff. Far from it! Upon closer inspection I see the names of girls listed in a column on the left, and on the right a price. Next to this price is another, higher figure, under which in brackets is written: "To take away."

1988: LIVING IN HIGH LITTLETON

On June 29, 1988, Archbishop Lefebvre consecrates four new bishops without papal approval, which strengthens the notion that he is a schismatic. If I were to follow him, would I be a schismatic too? One of my elder brothers declares to me over a glass of Burgundy: "Now that Lefebvre has gone too far, I expect you'll abandon toying with all this nonsense and embrace the official religion." I suppose I must appear to most people as a posturing drunk! However, I feel that I am subject to forces and inspirations which are beyond my control. A part of me prefers to live the life of a "country gentleman" and shun all interest in serious religion. Receiving the approval of my father is always high on my list of priorities, as is maintaining peace in my own household, but in spite of all this, I find myself creating arguments and causing much disapproval and unhappiness.

I have long abandoned the legal profession and have now set up as an independent financial adviser. I am now married with two young children.

My little office is in the attic of our spacious Victorian rectory and, as I sit at my desk surrounded by papers and files, I can just see out of the window in front of me. The view is of tops of trees which sway to and fro in the warm spring breeze. In the background, from two floors down, I hear the clatter of crockery and the wailing of a young child as Clare, my wife, clears up the breakfast things.

I summon up my courage with a large intake of breath, pick up the telephone receiver and dial the first number from my cold-calling sheet. I receive the response: "You have dialled an incorrect number." I tick off call number one on my pad. In conformity with the exhaustive sales training I received many years ago in London, I have to "pick up the telephone" twenty times every working day. This advice was from Trevor, my sales manager at Merchant Investors, now in jail for fraud, and I have more or less stuck to this routine, which ensures that the flow of potential customers does not dry up. "Once you have rung off, and no matter what has happened, don't stop to think about it, just go on to your next call," he said. I immediately tap out the next number and it's answered after two rings by a female voice:

"Howard Engineering, how can we help?"

I adopt my unique drawly upper-class accent, cultivated for cold calling:

"Good morning. May I speak to John Howard, please?"

"Who's that speaking, please?"

"Ahh...," I drawl, "this is Joseph Bevan."

"From...?"

"Ahh...yes...the Joseph Bevan Partnership..."

"Can I ask what's it about?" she asks, obviously smelling a rat. Now, I can hardly say what it is really about, can I? If I tell the absolute truth—that I want to try to sell him life assurance, investments, and pensions—she would most probably cut me off, and politely too. That would never do, so I reply:

"I think he'll remember me, just say the name, Joseph Bevan, it should be fine with him."

There's a short pause and then, finally:

"Hello, this is John Howard, do we know each other?"

This opening question from Mr Howard can be asked in a lighthearted and chatty way, which is excellent. Alternatively, he may speak in an impatient, brusque, and "time-is-money" way, which is not so good. But usually, my silver tones will normally elicit a positive and friendly response because when he hears me, the man may think that even if he can't place me, he is curious.

In answer to his question, I now tell my second white lie, which goes like this:

"We have a mutual contact in Geoff White of Whites Engineering, do you know him?"

I am careful not to say that Geoff White gave me Howard's name, that would land me in all sorts of trouble, because he did not. In fact, I have never met Mr White and all I have done is to look up the name of the nearest engineering company to Mr Howard's and dropped the name into the conversation.

I detect that Howard is relaxing and paying attention to me, even friendly now, so I decide that I can continue with my script. One of my most powerful phrases is: "I advise many engineering companies" (this was true) "but just because I can do things for them, which they're very grateful for, doesn't mean I can do anything for you." (Trevor always repeated, over and over again: "Don't oversell. Make them come to you and sound as if you're offering a service, but only to a select few.")

Finally, and this is the hardest part, we have to agree on a date when I can visit him. I always suggest two alternative dates which increases the chances that he will be available on one of them and, above all, I suggest a time of day which always sounds as though the meeting will be brief: "How about a quarter to eleven next Thursday, or ten to ten next Monday?" (Additionally, this sounds as though I am fitting Howard into a tightly packed schedule, which I am not.)

Salesmen have to maintain strict and comprehensive records of the process, otherwise they will lose track of their performance and, consequently, enter into lethargy. Lethargy is the greatest enemy of salespeople and can drive them out of the business. I have calculated that, over the years, for every three people I cold call, one will agree to meet me. This is an astonishing fact and has allowed me to expand my practice rapidly. The industry average is nearer to one appointment out of ten phone calls. For those sensible people who have refused to meet, I keep their details and renew my overtures a few months later. After all, his initial refusal to play ball may be attributed to a number of factors; perhaps he was just having a bad day, or else he was too distracted, it could be anything. Even when they are rude, I still don't give up because, sure enough, at my next approach he may be utterly charming.

I make my twenty phone calls and with some relief, as the process is always stressful, having to be at the peak of my wits for an hour, I pull on my work suit and trot downstairs.

1990: BUSINESS AND RELIGIOUS MATTERS

Having given Guy, the baby, a quick cuddle, I open the front door, step outside, and advance towards my car, only to be met by "Wibbly-Wobbly" who is strutting around in front of the house like a sentry and hoping for titbits from passers-by. This is an old mother goose which had been given to us by a lady in the village. A few visitors who would drive in are scared of this huge bird and often refuse to get out of their cars to approach the front door. They remain in their vehicles and sound the horn to summon attention from the house. In fact, the goose is a harmless old thing and even allows me to pick her up, always ensuring, of course, that I am not wearing my suit. The space outside the front of the house is the site of the daily goose patrol and the ground is covered with her dark green muck, causing everyone to tread carefully and necessitating frequent sweeping and hosing.

I drive out to my first meeting, which is at a haulage firm in Wells, about fifteen miles away. When I arrive there, it begins to rain. I park my car next to a row of lorries and the men standing around direct me towards the office of the managing director and owner, a Mr Ford. In actual fact, the office is no more than a portable cabin with two rooms—one for reception and the other for Mr Ford, who greets me from behind a desk covered in grimy piles of paper and files. The windows are filthy. Ford, wearing an oil-stained boiler suit, is short, rotund, and balding, with bushy grey sideburns. The room is full of cigarette smoke and half-drunk cups of coffee lie about. The carpet is threadbare, and I cross it to sit down on an office chair with a broken arm.

"So, what are yer sellin'?," he enquires curtly in Somerset dialect. As I hand him my card and start to explain, he interrupts with a wave of his hand and says curtly:

"I can't do business with you unless you have supped at the table of the Lord!"

Both Clare and I have been unhappy about our Catholic life to the extent that we are getting nothing out of Sunday Mass at our local parish and we are also uneasy about the position of the Church on a number of issues, including the teaching in schools. We're so incensed by the latest teaching aid, a teaching manual called *Weaving the Web*, that we get our letter of complaint published in the *Times* newspaper. It does no good, of course. Even though we regard ourselves as loyal Catholics, attending our local parish, we feel that the direction taken by the Church leaders is becoming more and more bizarre.

OUR CATHOLIC PARISH

At this stage we are going to Mass at the local parish of Midsomer Norton on Sundays; sometimes we go to Mass on Saturday evenings at a little Catholic church in Paulton, which is the next village to ours. Paulton is a satellite church of Midsomer Norton and both are run by the monks of Downside Abbey, which is in Stratton-on-the-Fosse, about ten miles away. Back to our anxieties about religion. I am developing a growing distaste for the current liturgy. Although I am a salesman, I just hate being sold to. At least, I don't mind people openly selling me things, but I cannot stand modern Catholic clergy doing it to me. The priests at Mass are always trying to curry favour and win the approval of their congregations, making us feel we are in the presence of a kind of ecclesiastical salesman. The church services are adjusted to fit the congregations: at Midsomer Norton, a beautiful converted mediaeval barn, we are treated to hymns and the occasional guitar Mass. For the more discerning upper classes, Downside Abbey lays on plainchant and sermons about touring the French vineyards and owning gîtes in the Perigord, all delivered beautifully and worthy of the best cold-callers.

I complain about this to my father when he comes to visit, and he replies on the lines of: "You don't go to Mass to be entertained." How many times have I heard that? But the point is that you *are* supposed to be entertained. That is the whole point of the post-Vatican-II Mass, isn't it? Modern seminaries train their young men to deliver the religion in such a way as to attract people along.

For the time being, we put up with everything, although I am increasingly becoming a bore. I do not spare anyone from my frustration, which is gradually turning to anger and resentment. When we entertain a monk from Downside, who happens to be our parish priest, I try to voice my concerns to him, but his response is a knowing smile and an indifferent shrug of the shoulders.

Let me state plainly that we have no religious observance in our household, although our increasing friendship with Father Lessiter is just about to change all that. If we have people to dinner, then—if they are important Catholics, for example—I intone grace in a very pompous voice.

CHAPTER 7

Growing Pains

1991: LIVING THE LIFE OF A GENTLEMAN

Although I feel that I am approaching a state of crisis as far as religion is concerned, I am very materialistic and, thanks to my growing income, have developed a love of certain luxuries. We have two cars in the drive and have joined the local stables to take riding lessons. We also take expensive holidays. We hire a castle on the banks of Loch Fyne for a week. Our wine consumption is impressive as we abandon supermarket fare in favour of the "Wine Society" and frequent a wine merchant in the next village. I make presentations at the meetings of the Wells Wine Society and can recite the names of all the Beaujolais vineyards. I am also greedy and put on weight as I indulge in splendid meals cooked by Clare. My father remarks during one of his visits: "Joe, you're living the life of a gentleman!"

When guests are present at our dinner parties, I begin to lose my politeness and reserve as the alcohol takes hold, and my religious anxieties begin to surface. Slanging matches frequently occur between me and those of my guests who take mild exception to my religious views.

I am following closely the activities of Archbishop Lefebvre and, having reacted initially with sympathy to the press reports that he is some kind of religious nutter, I am now becoming increasingly sure that he is on the right track. All his utterances seem to chime in with my own feelings and soon I become a "Lefebvre bore," suffering from, as one of my relations then put it, "Le-Fever"! My main difficulty with all this is that I do not know my Catholic faith and am easy prey to my intellectual superiors who are able to outwit me in argument, especially my father and father-in-law. My main arguments are more emotional than intellectual, and this results in many humiliations. I am unable to deal with the frequent accusations that I am disloyal to the Holy Father and thus "favouring schism." I am told that I am a Protestant because I am choosing my own preferences and not obeying the Pope. I really have no answer to this, but my instincts instruct me, deep down, that these people are wrong. My problem is that I just don't know why they are wrong, as I am not relying on prayer and study.

Clare is expecting our fourth child, and at the moment she is on the telephone. I can overhear her saying: "Yes, Father. That would be lovely!" She must be speaking to Father Lessiter, a traditional Catholic priest who has taken us under his wing and introduced us to the Latin Mass and the accompanying Catholic faith. Before his arrival we were—how shall I put it?—semi-lapsed modern Catholics who knew very little about the religion in which we were raised. When she has finished the call, Clare tells me that Father Lessiter is coming next day to offer Mass in our music room and to stay the night. By this time, we have an insatiable thirst for the Faith and the

Mass, both of which this priest has devoted his life to. Evangelising lost souls is what he does, and as far as that is concerned, he has a huge and growing flock all over the country and he wears out several cars in his missionary work. Father lives in Leicester and visits the West Country, where we live, once a month to see all the families who are recipients of his ministry.

We are usually attending the New Mass in our local parish and Dominic and Bridget, our eldest two children, are going to school at St Benedict's in Midsomer Norton, a Catholic primary school with an excellent headmaster, Peter Williams. As headmasters go, Williams is outstanding and he famously tells one of the parents: "If you refuse to believe everything your child says about our school, we won't believe everything they tell us about their home!" Every Thursday there is a Mass for the schoolchildren and their parents in the school hall. The priest stands behind a table upon which is draped a tatty blue cloth bearing the emblem of St Benedict's school. It is at one of these Masses, presided over by a monk from Downside Abbey who keeps on interrupting the service with little "jokes," that one of the smaller children pipes up: "Mum, this isn't a Mass, it's a shop!"

A GLIMPSE OF CATHOLIC LIFE

When Father Lessiter visits us shortly afterwards, he invites our eldest, Dominic, to attend his annual children's camp. We have never parted from any of our children up until now, and besides, Dominic is unfamiliar with the traditional Latin Mass, so we are hesitant. Nevertheless, at the appointed date in the early summer we pack him a small case, bundle him into the car, and off we go. Upon arriving at the large manor house set in the middle of a forest near Stroud, Gloucestershire, we see other cars arriving and disgorging little boys of a similar age to our son's. Father Lessiter advises us not to attempt to contact Dominic by telephone during the week of the camp, and that is hard for us. As we leave him with his case and drive away, we are full of foreboding: "What have we let ourselves in for?" The whole of the following week, we really miss Dominic and speculate as to all kinds of misadventures which might have happened to him.

On the last day of the camp, which is a Sunday, we have been invited to the final Mass before collecting Dominic. Upon arrival, we are directed to a large room on the ground floor which has been transformed into a chapel. As the children and parents gather, we have no sight of our son. Perhaps he's in hospital? A bell tinkles in the corridor outside and a procession enters the chapel, headed by a thurifer, acolytes and, finally, Father Lessiter dressed in gold vestments. We look again and discover that the boy holding the smoking thurible, and grinning from ear to ear, is our son, Dominic. To the side is a little electronic organ which is played expertly by a small boy. Everybody joins in with the singing, and the atmosphere is so devotional that we gulp with emotion. How I wish that the Pope could have been there and have seen for himself the incredible prayerfulness and serious piety of small boys as they witness what Father Faber described as "the most beautiful thing this side of heaven." How patronising are they who claim that children should be spared Latin because they cannot understand it.

CHAPTER 8

A Very Common Story

MY DEAR FRIEND OF MANY YEARS' standing, Jack, has asked to have his story related in this book and I am pleased to do so. Dating from 1993, it runs from here to page 97.

* * *

I am from a Catholic family which happily attended the Novus Ordo Mass in our local parish, some five miles away from our home, in Chipping Sodbury. My father regularly played the organ at Sunday Mass and Mum cleaned the church. My two sisters and I helped out with the singing which usually consisted of hymns, English congregational masses and, occasionally, plainsong. Our parish priest, Father Ignatius, had his eye on me from the start as he had noticed a seriousness and a piety which, he felt, pointed towards a priestly vocation. We rarely went to confession or anything like that, but I did notice how I had begun to take my prayer life seriously and started to read spiritual books as I became more involved in parish life.

When I turned eighteen Father Ignatius asked me to "do the readings" at Mass, only the first two, mind, as he himself always read the gospel. Owing to the slight reticence and, how shall I put it, reluctance on the part of the thinning congregation to help out during the services, we were left with me and my family singing, serving, and doing the readings. I was usually called upon to do the "bidding prayers," which Father Ignatius, who was trying to introduce changes, asked me to compose and which he quickly checked before the start of the Mass. He encouraged me to mention in the prayers anything which was topical, and much was made of any worldwide wars and famines in Africa. During these conversations I had with the priest, I couldn't help noticing his annoyance at being compelled by the bishop to make the liturgy more "dynamic." In the summer months, I would announce from the lectern: "Let us pray for all those who are away on holiday at this time..." and also: "We pray for Bishop Jim, who will be received in audience by the Holy Father next week." After each request, Father Ignatius would intone: "Lord, hear us!" and the reply would be muttered by all present: "Lord, graciously hear us!" One Sunday, Father read out the latest pastoral letter from Bishop Jim, which was on the subject of vocations. The bishop quoted a short passage written by a nun who recommended the religious life because "it was fun!" After reading out this last sentence, Father visibly winced and afterwards preached a sermon on how he wasn't surprised at the lack of vocations, which, he maintained, was caused largely by the search for "fun" on the part of those who generally trivialised the religious life.

AN INTERVIEW

Encouraged by the parish priest, with whom I had long interviews, I decided that I should meet the diocesan director of vocations to see if I had the requisite disposition to study for the priesthood. This was duly arranged and one day, I think it was a rainy Tuesday morning in July, I took a bus to the diocesan offices in Bristol. I sat for a while in a sitting room with a cup of coffee and studied back numbers of the *Tablet* until I was approached by a man in a tracksuit who held his hand out for me to shake. The letter inviting me to the interview was signed "Terry Dowding (Fr)" so I knew this was a priest and yet, as he stood before me, there was no physical clue as to his clerical state.

"Hello, Jack!," he said, "my name's Terry Dowding, good to see you. Come into my office and we can have a chat." His room was light and airy, but I was overwhelmed by the odour of tobacco. When we had sat down, he behind a large oak desk and me in a folding chair, facing him, he pulled out a packet of cigarettes and offered me one. I declined, being a lifelong non-smoker.

"Before we get down to business, Jack, I want to ask you, have you ever been involved with the Tridentine Mass or any such thing?"

"What is that?" I asked, mystified.

"Oh, you know, some people call it the Latin Mass, or the Old Mass. Surely you know about all that, don't you?"

I thought for a moment. "Well..." I started.

Father Terry sat bolt upright, his eyes widening. "Yes?"

"I've read news reports about Latin Mass people disobeying the Holy Father, but otherwise I have had no personal experience of any of that sort of thing."

The priest relaxed. "Well, thank the Lord for that! I thought we would just get that out of the way first."

Father Terry took a last deep drag of his cigarette and, as he blew out the smoke thoughtfully and crushed it into his saucer, he studied me.

"Jack, tell me, what exactly do you think the job of a priest is?"

I was expecting this question and had prepared my answer, thanks to some prior coaching by Father Ignatius.

"To save his soul and the souls of his flock."

Upon hearing this, Father Terry smiled, and this developed into a kind-hearted guffaw, followed by coughing and spluttering, common amongst heavy smokers.

"You don't *really* think that, do you?," he choked. "Someone's told you to say that, haven't they. Now tell me what you *really* think, Jack."

I pondered my reply, worried that my next answer would produce even more merriment, so I decided to play safe.

"I would love to hear your own views, Father, that's why I've come."

"Forget all this 'Father' nonsense, call me Terry."

Terry fished out another cigarette, lit it and blew out more smoke. My eyes were beginning to water.

"Jack, you can't do any good in the Church unless you address the *real* problems faced by *real* people who are in your care. Only after you have gained their trust and respect will they be prepared to open up and receive spiritual help. What's the use of telling a single mum, who is worried about paying her electricity bill or her rent, that she's not to worry because Jesus will save her? The life of grace and the striving for perfection is of no use to someone in prison for murder when you visit him."

"But how can I, as a parish priest, God willing, improve the lives of anybody?," I asked.

"You have to get involved in their lives. You do this by meeting as many people as possible, chairing committees, raising funds for the local school, marriage advice...the list is endless. You have to establish a public profile. Then the religious side will follow."

I was confused: "But I have no skills in all the things you've mentioned, all I can do is pray and study."

He was ready with his answer: "That's what they will teach you at seminary. Nowadays at least half of your training will be spent outside the college, and you'll be placed in a thriving working-class parish in a big city. After that, you will be bubbling with enthusiasm for your future work as a priest. Theology and canon law count for very little these days. Your priestly mission is ten percent knowledge and spirituality, and ninety percent *people*."

"I'm sorry to admit this, Father, but I'm naturally a very shy person."

"The seminary will teach you people skills, such as public speaking, how to deal with confrontational issues, and how to develop your personality. Seminaries nowadays place a lot of emphasis on psychology, and they even explore your inner sexuality. Have you ever slept with a woman, Jack?"

I was taken aback. "Certainly not!" I replied.

Quick on the uptake, Father Dowding was ready with his next aphorism: "I ask you, Jack, how can you love God if you've never loved a woman? You're not *gay* by any chance, are you?"

I was shaken by this question and, although I opened my mouth to reply, no words came out.

"Don't get me wrong, though. I wouldn't have minded if you were. It's just something the seminary has to be aware of. Of course, you're not *homophobic*, are you?"

"No, of course not!"

"Oh, that's good. We have to show love and tolerance towards people of all sexualities these days. When you go to seminary, they will carry out full psychosexual profiling for you, just to make sure that we have no skeletons in the cupboard."

Father Terry suddenly stood up and pushed back his chair. That was obviously the end of the meeting. I asked him what happens next, and he said that someone from the vocations department would write to me in due course and that I was not to worry as I was definitely "in."

JACK GOES TO THE ENGLISH COLLEGE

On the tenth of September, I alighted from the taxi at Via di Monserrato in Rome and lugged my heavy trunk to the ornate door of the Venerable English College. I rang the bell, which I could hear echoing inside. After waiting for a few minutes, I rang again and nobody answered, so I tried the latch, and the large oak door swung open. Upon entering I could see that there wasn't a soul about, in spite of my calling out, and so I sat on a bench and waited. After about ten minutes, I heard the sound of loud cheering and thumping and finally a door at the end of the hall was flung open and a crowd of young men emerged, all shouting gaily at the tops of their voices. One of the men approached me and exclaimed: "England won the rugby!" I made some gesture of acknowledgment, and he said: "C'mon, I'll show you the chapel."

As we entered the church, the first thing I noticed were two electric guitars which had been left on the back pew in perpetual adoration. Underneath the altar, really a table, was a mysterious gold box. I was told that it was time for "holy hour" and I was shown to my place where I sat down. I was wearing a dark suit but, as they wandered in, I noticed that most of the other young men seemed to be wearing shirtsleeves and jeans. There were about twenty young men, which was very few indeed, I thought. There were a few older men who were wearing clerical garb, but I saw no one in a cassock. I assumed that these men were the college professors. At supper later that evening, I noticed that there were about twelve round tables, nine of which were empty and lacked coverings, and I guessed that the number of students was relatively small. The holy hour consisted of some readings, a meditation and, finally, a student crooning at a microphone whilst strumming a guitar.

In spite of the small numbers of residents rattling around in a huge building designed to accommodate at least a hundred, I found the noise levels generally intolerable as pop music, which I loathe, echoed around the place and people seemed to talk in loud voices. At 10pm we were told not to make a noise, but the authorities seemed to have no problem with the students listening to their music on headphones. It was a very noisy place and the opportunity for quiet prayer and recollection was almost nonexistent and, if anything, discouraged. My parish priest, Father Ignatius, was here in the 1960s and he had described to me the seminary life in his day, suggesting that nothing had changed since then. The priest had warned me about "custody of the eyes," which meant that one normally went about one's business in a state of recollection and avoided looking other people in the eye. That custom was now nowhere to be seen. In actual fact the whole institution must have undergone such huge changes since his day that I was often left wondering whether it was really a seminary at all. The reason I say that is because great emphasis was laid on psychology, hours and hours of it, and often these sessions were supervised by a silvery-haired lady in a cardigan, who we were encouraged to address as "sister."

As the weeks went by, I befriended a seminarian who, like me, appeared to be disenchanted with the priestly training and our friendship started when he caught my eye during Mass, for as the guitar group had struck up with "Lord of the Dance," I definitely saw him rolling his eyes and smirking furtively. His name was Anselm and after holy hour one evening, Anselm invited me to his room for what he termed "a quick snifter." I was assured by him that it was perfectly okay for students to visit each other in their rooms and have a drink together. I wasn't so sure about this but didn't dare ask anyone about it.

"Have you ever attended a Tridentine Mass?" He asked lightheartedly, as we sipped our glasses of *Limoncello* in his bedroom. I said that I certainly had not, and he admitted that he, and a few others, occasionally sneaked off for a Friday evening Mass at Via Urbana, about half an hour's walk away. "You're welcome to come with us, but for God's sake, don't tell anyone!"

I shuddered at this idea as I wouldn't dream of being disobedient. But I was curious. Why was that the first thing Father Terry had been obsessed with during my interview? Surely it cannot be that bad.

"Think about it anyway," Anselm said. "I'm sorry to say this, but the truth is that a few of us can't stand the goings-on at the English College. So, rather than complain and get chucked out, we prefer to keep our heads down and hope to get ordained. Once that happens then they'll all be in for a huge shock! We are a growing number now, but we have to keep everything deadly secret. Almost like the life of a recusant priest in England during the sixteenth century."

"What else do you get up to, then?" I enquired.

"Usually, we meet up most evenings and pray the rosary or the breviary together."

"Breviary?" I asked. "What's that?"

"It's regarded as the heart and soul of priestly life. Before it was modernised and now fallen into disuse, every priest was obliged to say his breviary every day on pain of mortal sin."

"Mortal sin?" I exclaimed. "Never heard of it."

"Ho-ho!" exclaimed Anselm. "You've got a long way to go, haven't you? Have you never read a catechism?"

"You mean the Catechism of the Catholic Church?"

"No, I do not! That book is a watered-down sales manual for Vatican II. I'll lend you my Catechism of the Council of Trent if you like."

I hesitated at this, my friend adding: "Oh...never mind!"

I said: "My director of vocations in my diocese told me that the life of a priest is ten percent spirituality and ninety percent people."

"He said that, did he? The truth is that it's the other way round."

"How does that work?"

"Well, the purpose of seminary training is to fortify and prepare yourself spiritually for your priestly life through the grace of God. You do believe in God, I suppose?" he chuckled.

"Of course I do!" I exclaimed, reacting badly to his attempt at sarcasm.

"But do you *love* God?"

"Well...*love* is too strong a word..." I allowed my built-in English reserve to kick in; we are far too sophisticated to use such language.

"To be a priest you must not only love God, but you must also be *in love* with Him."

"How can I do that?"

"If you follow our routine of prayer, meditation, daily rosary, and the breviary, God will grant you the gift of love. But you must ask for it."

"How will I know when I'm *in love* with God, as you put it?"

"That's difficult," he replied. "I can assure you of one thing though. If you really love God, you will develop a horror of sin and...also...you'll hate the Novus Ordo Mass! There! I've said it!"

I was anxious. "I'm not sure I signed up for all that. I thought a priest was meant to make the world a better place by helping people."

"You sound like an ordination candidate in the Anglican Church. Perhaps you don't really have a vocation then." He replied gloomily. "Anyway, we'll see."

I had never met a "traditionalist" (as my father called them dismissively) until now and I can see why Father Terry was so cautious. Was my friend right, though? If so, then what am I doing here? I went to bed that night in an anxious state and, just before closing my eyes, there was a soft knock at the door. In walked Anselm, who chucked something onto my bed.

"This is a rosary plus a leaflet which will tell you how to say it. Goodnight!" And he was gone.

I was in a such a state of turmoil and indecision that I blurted it all out to the spiritual director who had been allocated to me. I was careful not to mention what my friend had labelled "hot topics." He was an elderly priest with a kindly twinkle in his eye, and he had no hesitation in his advice:

"Look here, Jack. You've not been here for five minutes and you're beginning to have doubts. That's all very normal and even healthy. We shouldn't take anything for granted. Just join in the life of the seminary with more commitment. Offer to do the readings at Mass, for example."

I left the spiritual director's room with a heavy heart. The "seminary life" to which he referred was becoming repellent as students vied with each other to be more and more progressive. Anyone showing reserve risked being labelled a "traditionalist" and could eventually be ejected. I assume this is why a number of the secret trads started to develop beards, grow their hair, and dress more shabbily, so as to establish their progressive credentials.

That night, and for no particular reason, I knelt down by my bed and, with the help of the leaflet, recited five decades of the rosary. As I did so, I meditated on the scenes of Our Lord's passion, as instructed by the paper in front of me. I slept well, having been overcome by an inner peace which I had never experienced before. The following morning, when I awoke, my mind was settled, and I knew what I had to do. After breakfast I sought out my friend Anselm and told him that I wished to attend their prayer meetings in his room. I also stated my intention to accompany his group to the Tridentine Mass on the following Friday evening. I could see that Anselm was elated, although he quickly adopted a serious expression.

"In God's name, not a word to anyone about this. If we're discovered, that will be the end of us," he whispered as he cast his eyes around, checking for eavesdroppers. From then on, I wholeheartedly participated in daily seminary life, being as helpful as possible. I even allowed a growth of stubble on my face so as to avoid suspicion. The craziest thing of all was that the more rebellious I became, in terms of objecting to any conservatism or promoting radicalistic ideas, the more the authorities approved of me and smiled on my deceptions. One of the hairier of my fellow students agreed to teach me how to play the guitar, and this met with universal approval on the part of the professors.

I can only imagine how an American citizen must have felt to enter a "speakeasy" for the first time during prohibition in the 1930s—that feeling of dread mixed with thrilling excitement as he took the plunge and broke the law for the first time. I had identical sentiments as I entered the Society of St Pius X chapel in Via Urbana that Friday evening. There were four in our little group, and we sat at the back. There were a few old ladies in front of us, who were praying the rosary out loud before Mass, and a mother struggled with two noisy toddlers. As I took my place on the wooden bench and looked up at the altar, I experienced a surge of happiness and relief. I had "come home," and yet, I had no idea until then where or what "home" was. All the nonsense, contradictions, worries, and doubts which had accumulated in my head over the years seemed to simply evaporate. I knelt down, or rather I collapsed down on my knees, a bell tinkled and in walked the priest with a young man wearing a black cassock and a cotta. No "good evening!" He started Mass facing the altar and was answered in whispers by the server. I was utterly overcome by the reverence and simplicity of the rite and when I rose to receive communion, I felt a touch on my elbow. I glanced at Anselm, who was next to me, and he said: "Not this time, I'll explain later." Not going to communion—why not? I was mystified because I was always told that not going to communion was a bit like being invited to a meal and refusing to eat anything.

As we emerged from the chapel into the street and made for a nearby bar, I noticed a man astride a stationary bicycle, who was watching us closely from inside the porch of a building nearby. He was bearded and I recognised him as one of our fellow students at college. I said nothing about this to my companions but had the certain feeling that the game was up for all of us.

You can guess the rest! We were summarily dismissed from the English College without even receiving the courtesy of an interview with the rector, which was a relief. We found on our return a note for each of us requesting that we vacate the building first thing the next day and, in the meantime, we were "excused" all activities.

The one thing I had learned from my short stay at the seminary was that I did not have a vocation to the priesthood. To be more specific, I knew that I was not called by God to the "sacrificing priesthood," which would make huge demands upon me, but rather my short life at the English College was preparing me for something completely different. The whole seminary system was designed to produce a generation of "ecclesiastical salesmen," like the Anglican ministry, and as I sat in the plane as it lifted off the runway at Rome airport, I knew that the whole idea of becoming a priest in the Novus Ordo Church had sunk with all hands. The effect of my first visit to the Tridentine Mass, though, was to clear my mind and banish all my lingering doubts, and for that I am eternally grateful to my confreres.

When I left seminary, I decided to qualify as a Chartered Accountant and went to live in London. I established contact with the Fathers of the London Oratory, who were most welcoming, and, finally, ended up going to Mass regularly with the Society of St Pius X.

(End of Jack's account)

CHAPTER 9

Life on the Farm

1995: COW MATTERS

We are now the proud owners of a large farmhouse with land, which is buried in the heart of the Somerset countryside outside Witham Friary. We have six children, plus a Jersey cow called Clarabel. In addition to the cow, we have a small flock of sheep, Wibbly-Wobbly is still with us, and there are two pigs. An assortment of hens, bantams, and ducks wander all over the grounds and are often subject to culls by our local friendly fox.

When we moved into our farmhouse in Witham Friary we converted a pleasant room on the lower ground floor into a proper family chapel. Father Lessiter kitted it out with everything we needed—vestments, altar linens, candles, and a tabernacle. The very first Mass he said in there was a requiem for the souls of all the previous owners of our new house. The reason for this was that Clare had seen a ghost of a lady in a long flowing dress climbing the staircase.

We have overextended ourselves by purchasing West Barn Grange with the assistance of a crippling mortgage and so, in common with the parents of most large families, financial problems are a constant worry.

Life on the Farm

Apart from a few weeks in the winter, when Clarabel is dry, I venture outside in my wellington boots twice a day and go to the cow shed with a milk bucket. Seated on a three-legged stool, taking care not to be lashed by her tail which is often covered in cowpat, I start to squeeze out the milk. Although the cow is tied loosely to an iron ring in the wall of the shed, I also have to ensure that she doesn't try to escape, and I do this by leaning into her with my head. Another of Clarabel's tricks is to suddenly raise a back leg and step into the milk bucket; the milk I have collected turns a brownish-green colour and has to be tipped away. Faced with all these potential hazards, I have to be on my guard and be ready to react quickly in order to avoid disaster.

I would describe my relationship with our Jersey cow as friendly, and I often take her for walks on a tether along the surrounding lanes where she munches the long grass growing on the verges. Unfortunately, I have a bruising encounter with the animal on one of these walks, as it is obvious that Clarabel has mistaken our friendship for something more serious. I let her tear up the grass contentedly and turn my back on her in order to admire the beautiful view. I am sitting on a grassy bank and suddenly feel a thump on my left shoulder, and then my right shoulder as she tries to mount me. In my panic, with this huge animal bearing down on me, and feeling her hot grassy breath in my right ear, I manage to roll away from her down the bank, and land in the middle of a hawthorn hedge. The news of this incident causes much merriment in my family and, ultimately, the whole village gets to hear of it. Later, over a pint of cider in the Seymour Arms: "How's yer girlfriend then, Joe!," someone shouts over the bar, to gales of laughter from some cider-soaked farm labourers. I am advised by a seasoned farmer never to turn my back on an animal, especially horses, cows, and sheep.

One evening in the spring, I am at home and in charge of the children as Clare has gone out to play the oboe in a concert. I am supervising their tea and they're all sitting down happily munching. Noticing the time of day, I announce that I will have to leave them alone as it is time to milk Clarabel.

"Now look," I say to them, "I have to pop out to milk the cow and leave you for a moment." There is a large bell on the side, and I point to it, saying: "If anything happens and you need me urgently, just go outside and ring this bell." I put on my overalls and boots, grab the bucket, and start out for the field. I am soon extracting the milk as I crouch down on the stool when, suddenly, the bell rings. It rings and rings so, in a panic, I drop everything and dash back to the house. I behold Rupert standing in the drive, his thumb in his mouth and the other hand still ringing the bell.

"What on earth has happened?," I enquire.

"Peter's being silly!" comes the reply.

DRESSING UP

From their earliest years, our children have dressed up in homemade vestments and performed pretend Masses at home. Every empty breakfast cereal packet is cut out and turned into a mitre and every strawberry punnet is painted black and transformed into a biretta. When our favourite cat is found dead, it is buried by the children who wear black vestments, sing the requiem, and process solemnly to the burial site in the vegetable garden, carrying the dead cat which has been placed into a miniature coffin.

Many years ago, when I was living at home, we entertained a married couple who brought with them their two young boys. The family weren't Catholics but Church of England, and they lived in a cathedral city and the two boys sang in the cathedral choir. My youngest brother, Ben, aged eight, decided to stage one of his usual pretend Masses, and he donned his homemade vestments, which included a bishop's red skull cap which my brother Tony had acquired from his seminary at Oscott. All the parents were present, plus a few of us children, as Ben processed in with cope and mitre. Not to be outdone, the two little boys took over the service and turned it into a very low church affair with lots of readings from the Book of Common Prayer. Ben's confusion was complete, and an undignified scuffle broke out at the altar (a table in the sitting room) as a battle for liturgical supremacy took place.

On the first of November, the feast of All Saints, Clare and I organise a fancy-dress competition where the children dress up as their favourite saints and this has become an annual event. If a priest is with us, either Father Lessiter or Father Crowdy, they would guess the name of the saint and the winner is the child who represents the best likeness.

"Perhaps I too should dress up as my favourite saint?," I suggest lightheartedly. Back comes the answer from one of the children: "Oh, Daddy, you wouldn't need to dress up!" I am bowled, middle stump.

BAZIL

The children are all too young to be of any help on our small farm so most of the work is carried out by me, assisted by Clare who is also running the home school. I do have help and advice, often unasked for, from a nomadic local Somerset farmhand who has adopted us. His name is Bazil Francis, and he comes almost every day to offer advice and assistance. Bazil, known in the village as "Baaz," is a cider alcoholic who spends a lot of time in the local public house, the Seymour Arms. Baaz is a heavy smoker and lights up one cigarette after another. Consequently, he has a very deep throaty speaking voice and what I term a graveyard cough. This cough is so loud, continuous, and penetrating that we are all concerned about his general health. Baaz is arrested by the Avon and Somerset police for driving his car without insurance or MOT. Had the traffic cops bothered to breathalyse him they would have discovered a high concentration of alcohol in his blood, thanks to a boozy evening in the Seymour Arms. But I assume that, as they know exactly who he is, they refrain from carrying out this final humiliation. When he appears at Wells magistrates' court, he pleads guilty to all the charges, and I am called upon to make a plea in mitigation for him. I wax lyrical about the "twilight"

Life on the Farm

and "nomadic" world of Somerset peasants who allow the reality of everyday life to pass them by. "He is not a criminal and there isn't an ounce of guile in his makeup," I intone. The defendant gets away with a £30 fine, to be deducted from his social security payments. All rather pointless, I decide. After the hearing we are sitting in the bar of the Star Hotel, opposite the courthouse, Baaz is a bit grumpy and pulls a long face.

"What's the matter, Baaz?," I enquire.

"You made me feel very small and idiotic in that court," he replies.

He is right about this. But I think to myself how else Baaz and his friends run roughshod over the law. His Social Security claims are definitely fraudulent, as I know that he has all sorts of other income. He probably neglects his two teenage children, and his wife walked out on him years ago. He describes to me all kinds of ventures he undertakes which seem to consist mainly of pilfering from the well-off in order to give to penniless farmhands—a sort of agricultural Robin Hood.

A SIGN OF HOPE

One of my elder brothers, who is a regular visitor, questions me about Bazil: "Joe, your religion is all very well, but if you're trying to get you and your family to heaven, what about Bazil? Is it your position that he, and most people like him, will go to hell because they aren't Catholics and have never heard of the Traditional Latin Mass?" I struggle with this question because, up until now, I have always separated my religious beliefs from my day-to-day life. So what *does* happen to "normal" people when they die? Firstly, it is definitely not my place to condemn people to hell, that is obvious. On the other hand, what can one do about the millions of people who are not religious? I decide that, during my daily prayers, I should pray for all those whom I come into contact with and leave them to the justice and mercy of God. I assume that these people, like Bazil, are a million miles from religion of any kind.

A few months later, we are given a beautiful statue of Our Lady which I install in the garden, overlooking our vegetable patch. Bazil sees the statue and immediately sets to work, painstakingly constructing a wooden shelter for it and planting roses. He displays such dedication that both Clare and I suspect supernatural forces at work.

Later in the year I receive a message from Bazil's ex-wife that he is in hospital with chronic bronchitis and isn't expected to live. I arrive at the hospital and the nurse shows me into the ward, where I see Bazil lying in bed attached to an assortment of tubes. He is barely conscious. I am suddenly inspired to remove the brown scapular from around my neck. "Bazil," I say, "I want to put this around your neck, and you must promise not to allow anyone to remove it." He nods keenly and I place the scapular over his head. The next day I am informed that he died peacefully during the night. This is a miracle and, as a result, I feel sure that Bazil is saved but subject, no doubt, to a long stretch in purgatory. Who knows?

A WORD ABOUT FUNERALS

At every funeral, as Catholics we know that there is some doubt lingering over the soul that once animated the cold body in front of us in the coffin. I have attended Novus Ordo funerals, such as that of my own godmother, where the celebrant, clad in white vestments, tries to reassure those relatives who are present that the deceased has gone to heaven, having led a blameless life. Not only is this a false supposition, but it is by no means any sort of comfort to the bereaved. Worst of all, the purpose of the modern funeral Mass is not to pray for the soul of the deceased but, rather, to celebrate his or her life. I have even seen close friends of the dead person trailing up to the front to address the congregation in glowing terms about the departed, even cracking jokes such as "we all remember his wicked sense of humour and he's probably laughing with us now." On one occasion a mourner stated that the deceased was a wine lover, and he went on to describe their tours of French vineyards, and how they frequently got legless together.

Here is an excerpt from the guide to funerals published by the diocese of Leeds in 2021: "Every aspect of a Catholic funeral rite expresses these fundamental beliefs. It is an opportunity to thank God for the gift to us of the life of our departed loved one and, with the aid of our prayers, to send them on their journey to new life with Him." Are we now expected to believe that everyone goes to heaven? It certainly looks that way. The words of Our Lady to the children at Fatima come to mind, where she said that many souls go to hell because there is no one to pray for them. This is a tragedy. If there is now no doubt about the salvation of the deceased's soul, then why bother to have a funeral Mass at all? The answer to this lies in the desire of the modern Church, with its reformed funeral service, merely to celebrate the life of the departed person and, above all, to comfort the mourners who are present. Neither of these objectives have anything to do with the Catholic faith and, in any case, are more or less futile.

One of the stirring features of the Catholic Church before Vatican II was that, unlike everyone else, Catholics did not fear death and talked about it quite openly. For a person who is in a state of grace, the transformation from life to death is a brief and effortless process. Nowadays, thanks to the watering down of the theology, death is regarded by Novus Ordo Catholics in the same way as it is by most other people—with fear and trepidation.

So, I had prayed for the saving of Bazil's soul and, before the end, in spite of his life without God, he made a final gesture of faith by receiving the brown scapular from me. Any tiny and almost insignificant act, such as his, may well be sufficient to ultimately save a soul.

CHAPTER 10

Life Under Fire

1997: A DISTRACTION

Jack is a thoughtful man, about ten years younger than I, who often visits us here, in Witham Friary. It was during one of these visits that he described his experiences at the English College as a seminarian (see chapter 8). He is unmarried and, having abandoned any thought of getting ordained, has since qualified as a Chartered Accountant and works for a small firm of accountants in London. During our interminable and often nocturnal conversations, I value his insight into most issues, religious or otherwise, and am always amused by his gift of "make-believe" as he paints imaginary verbal pictures to illustrate the points he is making. So it is that on long country walks along muddy lanes and farmland or facing each other in the public bar of the Seymour Arms, he escapes into his revelry and develops his imaginary world and invents more characters who inhabit it. Jack has a very slow and dreamy way of speaking which commands my attention as he manifests his enormous talent for word-painting. Clare has no time for such trifles as she complains that Jack is a distraction, liable to lead me astray, as I often neglect my fatherly duties when I'm in his company.

I would like to give the reader some idea of the characters whom Jack has invented over the years to illustrate his views, particularly on religious matters. There is a young married couple to whom Jack often refers, Jeff and Lydia. According to Jack, Jeff and Lydia are a professional couple with two teenage children who are generally rebellious and ghastly. Above all, they are comfortably off as they both work full time, and the children are farmed out to boarding schools. Jack always refers to Jeff and Lydia when he needs to illustrate what he terms the "materialism" of the modern age. They will fail to comprehend any possible spiritual or philosophical side to the problems they face in their daily lives, and these difficulties arrive in legions. Above all, Jeff and Lydia deny the existence of Divine Providence and rely entirely on their own efforts as they attempt to accumulate more and more wealth which, they assume, will give them the happiness which, so far, has eluded them.

One of the most interesting features of this unhappy couple, Jack explains, is the subject of family holidays. When they went to Majorca last year, the couple admit that they *were* happy. As they plan their excursion for next year, they maintain how happy they *will* be as they excitedly make plans for their "holiday of a lifetime" in Greece. At this very moment, though, they are on a dream holiday in Tenerife and all is not well. The children are bored and resentful ("we miss our friends back at home") and generally rebellious. The hotel has an air-conditioning system which keeps the family awake at night and tempers are frayed during the daylight hours. Jeff and Lydia's hotel room is stuffy, and yet they cannot open the windows owing to the stench arising from the kitchen waste bins which are just outside. On their return journey, they are held up at the airport for six hours and have to sit in the middle of a throng of likewise angry travellers. They arrive home to find the front door smashed in and a note from the police lies on the kitchen table. They discover that burglars have visited and gone selectively through the whole house stealing the jewellery. Jack says that, after returning home, Jeff and Lydia will soon forget about the very real miseries which their holiday entailed and will convince themselves that it was a wonderful holiday. They will only recall the few good times such as a nice meal, glorious sunshine, and the scuba diving. All memories of the disasters will be airbrushed out of their consciousness. Jack goes on to mention that their last "dream" holiday was no better and yet, as time passes, that trip takes on the mantle of perfect bliss in their memories.

The point of this sorry tale, Jack maintains, is that Jeff and Lydia will never be happy. They eventually tumble to the conclusion that on holiday, they are pretty miserable, and that on their last holiday they were also miserable. The holiday of a lifetime in Greece, which they are currently planning, may not be the blissful experience which they are seeking and, eventually, they come to realise that they can never be happy. This is because they are confusing pleasure, which is short-lived, with happiness, which is permanent. The sadness is that they are seeking happiness in all the wrong places as it is only available through union with Our Lord. As Jeff and Lydia slowly come to the realisation that they can never be happy, depression will set in, and they may start to avail themselves of the services of "counsellors" or, more likely, the bottle. In this way, Jack displays his masterfully "doom 'n' gloom" outlook on everything.

Jack and I have lengthy discussions centred upon a multitude of wide-ranging subjects, especially the current controversies surrounding the crisis in the Catholic Church. One subject, which particularly exercises us, is the prevalence of diocesan priests who say both the Latin (Tridentine) form of Mass and, at the same time, have no problem saying the Novus Ordo Mass. It happens that we know of several people, followers of the Society of St Pius X, who will never attend a Latin Mass said by a priest who also says the New Mass. My friend and I are frequently exercised by this dilemma and disagree in our conclusions, as I will never miss Mass even if it means going to one said by a priest in a state of compromise.

Jack is staying with us over a weekend in the summer and we have just returned from the SSPX Mass in Bristol. After a late lunch, Clare suggests that I take Jack and some of the children in our nine-seater to visit the steam railway museum at Cranmore, about ten miles away. This is a favourite destination for our youngsters and off we go. Jack is sitting in the front passenger seat next to me and he is speculating dreamily about the latest imaginary problems faced by Jeff and Lydia. Having pulled into the museum car park, the children get out and run off, promising to be back at the minibus at an agreed time for our return journey. I keep hold of the youngest who is in a push chair. As we wander around the host of steam engines on display, Jack says, all of a sudden: "If you knew that the driver of this steam engine also drove diesel engines, would you travel on it?" Back and forth goes our slightly fantastical conversation until Jack admits that the Beeching reorganisation in the early 1960s (Lord Beeching closed down most of the unprofitable railways and signalled the demise of the steam locomotive) was the same disaster as the Second Vatican Council was for Catholics. I betray my liberalism by stating that, although admittedly steam trains are superior to diesel trains, yet I see no problem in travelling on either, and with a clear conscience too. When the children meet us at the minibus, I drive us all home to the accompaniment of Jack stretching the diesel and steam analogy as far as he can and becoming even more ridiculous by doing so.

Shortly afterwards I am back home, sitting in my favourite armchair and scanning the Sunday newspaper when I am summoned to the telephone. I put the receiver to my ear and a rather bossy male voice says:

"Mr Bevan?"

"Yes?"

"This is the Avon and Somerset police; we've been summoned to the Cranmore Railway Museum. We're holding two of your children, Peter and Gervase. You left them behind and they're very upset!"

1998: FRENCH SCHOOLS: A TOE IN THE WATER

The final piece in the family jigsaw is our children's schooling. For the past three years we have homeschooled our eldest offspring but realise that this is not ideal for youngsters who may feel cooped up in a hothouse. Our overall desire is to ensure that we create conditions which will allow them to lead happy and holy lives and thus save their souls. Above all they must come to see Catholic Tradition as normal, even "cool." Here in the United Kingdom, they hardly see any other traditional Catholic friends as we are all so spread out. This is why we send them to boarding schools in France, run by the priests of the Society of St Pius X, and also, for the girls, a convent school run by the Dominican nuns. The traditional Catholic movement in France is massive. In Paris, for example, whole apartment blocks are filled with "tradis." An additional advantage of sending our children to France is that they can become bilingual and will at least be able to get jobs on Eurotunnel and the cross-channel ferry.

In the autumn our eldest three children, Dominic, Bridget, and Guy, travel to the French schools and the immediate results are traumatic. There they are, knowing little or no French, thrust into an utterly foreign world of coldness, damp, and homesickness. Clare and I had rarely parted from our offspring before, and I visit their empty bedrooms at home with a lump in my throat. Very shortly we receive a letter, in French, from one of the priests at Camblain informing us that our children are dirty and sulky. He hints that we should abandon the French project as our children show no signs of settling in.

As Clare and I are already in a state of heightened nervousness and anxiety, we regard this as, perhaps, a sign from God to take our offspring back to England. Thanks to the advice of another English mother, seasoned in the French system, we decide to hold our nerve. Our friend advises us not to reply to the letter and just carry on as if nothing has happened. A few days later we receive another letter from a priest friend who has just visited the school on his travels. "I have seen your boys and can confirm that they are happy and are well settled in," he writes. We breathe a huge sigh of relief at this and when we revisit the school a few weeks later, the priest who originally complained to us is charming and smiley. He has forgotten all about his letter.

1999: WE KICK OVER OUR SANDCASTLE

With our eldest three children settled in France, we send the next in age, Rupert, to Camblain. Rupert is eight years old, and he starts in the summer term at the end of the academic year. There is a good reason for this as he spends the initial time getting familiar with his new surroundings and learning some French. He is not required to do any formal schoolwork and when we collect him for the weekends, he has a blackened face and reeks of woodsmoke. He spends most of his time helping with the school bonfire, which is always alight, and playing games. Abbé Berteaux is always busy with building projects, digging trenches and laying pipes, so all the youngsters help him. There is a collection of animals also, goats and donkeys, which they all help tend. We don't have to worry so much about Rupert as his elder brothers keep an eye on him.

So, here we all are, living in the Somerset countryside, which is as close to paradise as one could wish to be. But it cannot be God's will for us to create heaven on earth. It is almost second nature for human beings to pamper themselves by working all out for earthly happiness and the accumulation of worldly possessions. And yet happiness is not to be found in any of these things because, like Jeff and Lydia, we are looking in the wrong places. We are now so far away from our children's schools that we have to take action. Above all, we do not want to lose touch with them as the schools all take a dim view of distant and absentee parents. The trips to France are becoming very burdensome and, because we have to cross England via congested motorways in order to reach the English channel, we must act. So, sure enough, God provides us with a choice: either take the cowardly way out and stay in our beautiful house surrounded by animals, or give it up for the sake of the ultimate happiness and sanctification of the family. And that means moving as near as possible to France so as to be nearer our children. Kent—here we come!

The employment of a firm of builders who have been renovating West Barn Grange over the years has resulted in a massive increase in our debt burden. We feel that the level of debt is becoming unsustainable and our money problems are getting out of control. Additionally, my financial advice business is suffering from diminishing returns because there are just not enough potential clients to keep me going

Life Under Fire

and I am having to travel further and further afield in order to seek prospective customers. Property prices, we notice, are considerably cheaper in East Kent than they are in Somerset, especially in Dover, where nobody in their right mind would want to live. The decision to turn our backs on Somerset is not easy and is the result of countless prayers and novenas, especially to St Joseph. In the end, though, we are fortified by our prayers, and the decision is obvious; we now have the confidence to see this project through, and all our doubts are removed. Yet all the advice we receive from our friends and relations, both asked for and unasked for, is negative: "You're crazy!"

BEWARE OF LAWYERS

Having made this momentous decision, we make a couple of trips to East Kent to find a suitable property for our large family. Eventually we have our offer accepted on a former old people's home in Park Avenue, Dover, which has a basement room that would be ideal as a chapel. Now starts the arduous task of packing up our Somerset house and I hire a skip into which is tipped many non-essential items. There is a huge amount of furniture, much of which has been in the family for generations, some of which we have to give away, as our next house is too small to accommodate it. The man who is buying West Barn Grange has a solicitor handling his purchase whom I can only describe as a "tartar" and straight out of *Bleak House* by Charles Dickens. Perhaps all solicitors are like him nowadays, yet his delaying tactics and other activities, all clearly designed to force us to lower the agreed price, almost makes us withdraw from the sale. I am thankful that I never qualified as a solicitor. It seems to me that underhanded tactics and the pursuit of advantages, however insignificant, appear to be the stock-in-trade of modern lawyers. It is the interminable "nitpicking" which most depresses us.

Finally, on a date in November, we set off for Dover along with three removal vans. Clare takes the small car with ten-day-old Jean-Baptiste, our ninth child; she is the advance party and plans to pick up the keys to our new house from the agent in Dover. I follow with the rest of the children. Later that day, I am feeding the older children in a motorway café when Clare rings me. She has been sitting outside the new house for three hours and cannot gain admittance until the purchaser of West Barn Grange has entered that property and is satisfied that all is well. This is thanks to expert advice from his lawyer, who was hanging on to the completion money until the very last moment. I know enough to suggest, perhaps unkindly, that a few more pounds will be paid to the lawyer's client account in interest, thanks to this rather spiteful manoeuvre.

I am reminded of similar difficulties when we sold our house in High Littleton in 1991. On that occasion, the purchaser informed us that he would only go ahead with the transaction if we left him our lawnmower. My advice to those unfortunate people who try to sell their houses is never take your house off the market until exchange of contracts. You must carry on showing prospective purchasers around your property. Otherwise, your purchaser and his lawyer, seeing that you are committed to selling to him, will usually start to play silly games with the agreed purchase price.

"And he said, Woe unto you also, ye lawyers! for ye lade men with burdens grievous to be borne, and ye yourselves touch not the burdens with one of your fingers" (Luke 11:46).

2002: I GO TEETOTAL

On the sixth of June this year, after much agonizing, indecision, and false starts, I finally abandon my consumption of alcohol. I have made countless attempts in the past to give up the booze and the season of Lent was my preferred time for complete abstinence. It was always torture, though, as I counted the days until either a feast day, such as St Joseph's on March 19, the Annunciation on March 25, or Easter itself. Almost every day in Lent I would scan the liturgical calendar for an excuse to imbibe. Now that I have given up for life, I find that, having nothing to look forward to, the inconvenience is slight, and I never pine for a glass of wine. There is just one caveat to that bold statement, and it is this: I hope that heaven is well stocked with Somerset cider which, like the Tridentine Mass, is the most beautiful thing on earth. I have fond memories of visiting a famous model railway with the children, which was constructed in the back garden of a retired gentleman who lived in Bruton, a local town. He offered me a glass of his homemade cider which I reluctantly accepted, as I had often tasted such privately produced beverages with mixed results. I needn't have worried. The golden liquid slid down my throat and I tasted the bittersweet of Cox's Orange Pippin apples. I remember little about the return journey back to our house!

A NEW RESPONSIBILITY

I am approached by the superior of the Society of St Pius X and asked if I would take charge of the annual SSPX pilgrimage from Rochester to Canterbury, which normally takes place at the end of July. I have already attended a couple of these events with my older children and found them to be disorganised and deliberately "penitential." There were usually about sixty pilgrims, mostly young men, and very few children. This is because the food was awful, the facilities were disgusting (one lavatory only), and the evening camping was sometimes dominated by a group of neofascists, one of whom recited the speeches of Adolf Hitler for entertainment. Something had to be done!

My task, as I see it, is to develop the Canterbury Pilgrimage into a proper family event and, above all, to make it "child-friendly." The main priority is to make this pilgrimage the main social and spiritual event of the year, there being preciously few others to speak of, and I invest some of my own money into this project. My initial objective is to allow the pilgrims better food and toilet provisions. My wife, Clare, helps organise the catering with a team of helpers. I co-opt a committee of youngsters from our local Mass centre in Herne to whom I delegate all the main tasks, such as advertising, marshalling, first aid, and organising the campsite. I order some mobile toilets to deal with the other difficulty.

The opening Mass in our first campsite is a sung Mass, with the choir consisting of my children and some of their friends. Already I can see an overall improvement in morale as the pilgrims feel that the whole pilgrimage is well organized to the smallest detail. As the years go by, we shed the nucleus of fascist hard-drinkers, who are discouraged by the new atmosphere of religious fervour as opposed to the political sectarianism which had hitherto seemed to prevail.

2008: LIFE IN FRANCE

We now have ten children and have been living, since 1999, in a large house in Dover. Having left behind our farm with its animals, I still have panic attacks in the middle of the night, imagining that I haven't shut up the chickens or, worse still, I have not fed the pigs for nine years.

We divide our time between Dover and our apartment in Guise, northern France, which we visit every other weekend in order to meet up with most of our children who are at French schools. These fortnightly visits give them a taste of home life and its comforts. After we cross the channel to France, we first call in at the boys' school in Camblain-l'Abbé and collect them. We take this opportunity to chat to the priests and staff to make sure that all is well. We know that it is essential to maintain close contact with the school in order to nip in the bud any problems which our children may be facing. Having collected the boys we proceed to the girls' convent in Le Herie, which is near our apartment at Guise. It is inevitable that our children bring their friends for the weekend who, no doubt, have heard about the high standard of English cuisine available at "Château Bevan." Our French friends joke about our apartment, and I have been christened by them "Le Duc De Douvre." Our seventeen-seater minibus is therefore packed to the gunnels with French and English children plus all their suitcases, which are stuffed with dirty washing.

On Sundays, when in France, we all go to early morning Mass at the girls' school at Le Herie where we listen to the Dominican nuns singing. I have never heard unaccompanied plainsong sung so beautifully; but of course, they are not just singing, they are praying. The simplicity of the sound is sufficient to raise hearts and minds up to Almighty God, which is the whole point of plainsong. We have become accustomed, in England, to plainchant choirs being unable to resist swelling on phrases and generally overdoing it, thereby presenting a distraction to the congregation. At Le Herie, the singing of the nuns is in complete harmony with the priest at the altar in a seamless tapestry. Driving back home to our French apartment, we stop off at the "boulangerie artisan" which sells croissants and bread for our late breakfast, at which we stuff ourselves with these beautifully fresh and crispy-light foodstuffs, smeared with homemade jam.

The convent is in northern France, the towns are ugly and industrialised, and the agriculture concentrates on the intense farming of sugar beets. During the cold and wet autumns our minibus is invariably stuck behind a procession of muddy lorries and tractors, all hauling mountains of

Life Under Fire

"*betteraves*," as the French call them, to the local factory for processing into beet sugar. Near the girls' school is a town by the name of Origny-Sainte-Benoite, which my children have nicknamed "Smelligny." This is where the muddy transports make for, with their loads of beets which have been collected from huge piles at the roadside by the farms. A visit to this place will be rewarded by an overpowering sweet, sickly, cabbagey smell which pervades the whole area, as tall factory chimneys belch copious clouds of white vapour into the atmosphere. It reminds me of Mordor, as described in *The Lord of the Rings* by J. R. R. Tolkien.

There is no doubt that northern France is a grim part of the country, especially during autumn and winter, and it often lowers our spirits. Most of the inhabitants are poor and of short stature and wear faded sports clothing. Guise itself, where we spend our weekends, has narrow streets and tall houses in a style more common in the Low Countries. These streets contain mainly dilapidated and boarded-up shops. The huge and rather beautiful Catholic church there is usually locked up as indeed are most of the churches in the area. We once entertained a local clergyman to tea and he confirmed that Catholicism was at a low ebb, with perhaps up to fifteen parishes amalgamating under a solitary and elderly presiding priest. Much of this area was laid waste by the guns of the first World War as huge military cemeteries are dotted around the landscape and we hear stories about farm vehicles in the fields being blown up, having run over unexploded ordnance.

At the boys' school at Camblain-l'Abbé there is a collection of bullets and shell cases in the headmaster's office whilst, amongst the boys, there operates an underground black market of war souvenirs. Our children and their friends gleefully show us their collections of field bandages, cartridges, and cap badges. The school grounds are scarred by artillery barrages from which huge water-filled holes and craters are the remaining evidence. The school buildings themselves remind me of a shanty town, being of poor quality, sprawling over a wide area. They are single floor only. The sleeping quarters for one-hundred-and-fifty-or-so boys are leaking and poorly heated so that all the bedclothes, and indeed, the clothes which they wear, are damp much of the time.

Nobody cares about any of these minor inconveniences because, thanks to the energetic and apostolic headmaster, Abbé Berteaux, the pupils receive the milk and honey of a proper Catholic education. The condition of the buildings, combined with the daily routine and the first-class teaching, turn the boys into real men. Abbé Berteaux, along with some of the other priests, is ex-army and the whole school is run on military lines with parades, assault courses, and, on Fridays, a ceremony where the whole community stands outside in formation to witness the running down of the school flag to the accompaniment of a lone trumpeter. The school at Camblain-l'Abbé bears no comparison with my old school at Downside, where there was a hierarchy of senior boys, culminating in school prefects who dressed, and often behaved, like wedding guests, the head boy residing in a small flat with his friends. Camblain has no prefects and, even for those in their final year (some of whom are over nineteen years old), they have to muck in with the rest in the cold and damp dormitories.

A HAPPY SCHOOL

Walking through the front door of Camblain, I am immediately assailed by the combined smells of socks, French cooking, and Gitanes cigarettes. The school chapel, however, is quite beautiful and is my first port of call whenever I visit. As I kneel in front of the Blessed Sacrament, I always give thanks for the massive graces which we have received, particularly this haven of truth, order, and beauty which the school encapsulates. I cannot adequately convey the experience of a truly happy school. One of the most effective methods of keeping discipline on an even keel is the *"binômage"* system. This operates in such a way that every senior boy is personally responsible for the behaviour and overall welfare of a junior. If a junior misbehaves in some way, not only is he punished, but also the senior who was his responsibility. Punishments usually consist of detention or the withdrawal of some privilege or other. There is definitely no corporal punishment in the school as it is quite unnecessary. On a burnished wooden board in the school hall there is a list of names of boys. These are not Oxbridge scholarships or cricket captains but, rather, those who have been ordained priests.

CHAPTER 11

Working It Out

2009: INTRODUCING... MR GOOGLE-BRAIN

Family conversation around the dinner table is usually of a high quality. The most common subject under discussion is religion, of course, and I never fail to be impressed by the knowledge displayed by my children, owing to the excellent standard of the religious education they receive at their French schools. I would hasten to add that some of the content is way above my paygrade and I am sometimes unable to contribute anything useful to the discussion as some of my offspring display deep theological insights. It is marvellous to observe the power of logical argument and the willingness of the participants in a debate to give way and acknowledge the force of an argument when it is presented to them. Much to the annoyance and irritation of my offspring, who regard many of my opinions as homespun, I have invented a character who inhabits our modern world, and his name is Mr Google-Brain. Google-Brain and his millions of disciples possess much general knowledge and are expert at pub quizzes. Unfortunately, they lack any inclination towards analysis and critical thought of any kind. Such is the condition of most people today.

I know several Google-Brains personally, and they also dominate the airwaves and most types of social media. The main characteristic of such people is to accept without question the universal narratives of progress and de-Christianisation. Such is their lack of introspection, owing to their deep attachment to electronic media, that they think, and speak, in slogans.

Google-Brain simply rejects the existence of miracles, such as the feeding of the five thousand, as he possesses no belief in the supernatural, and explains it away on the grounds that all Our Lord did was to encourage people to share their picnics. The miraculous healings at Lourdes, which are professionally and independently verified, are likewise disposed of by means of a plain denial. And yet what is so ridiculous is that the disbeliever in the miraculous unquestionably accepts daily miracles in human life such as the birth of a child. He takes for granted the fact that his heart continues to beat, year in and year out, in spite of his regular assaults on it through the use of drugs, tobacco, and alcohol. As for the resurrection? No thank you! Indeed, one has only to lift a quotation from a treatise by Cardinal Müller, printed in Germany in 2010, to show how even one of our most conservative prelates fights shy of proclaiming the greatest miracle of them all: "A running camera would not have been able to make an audiovisual recording of either the Easter manifestations of Jesus in front of his disciples, nor of the Resurrection event, which, at its core, is the consummation of the personal relation of the Father to the incarnate Son in the Holy Ghost."[1]

---

[1] Gerhard L. Müller, *Katholische Dogmatik*, 8th ed., p. 300.

DOES GOD EXIST?

Even though the arguments for the existence of God have a lot going for them, Mr Google-Brain offers no counter-arguments apart from "let's agree to disagree." Of course, God being eternally merciful wants people to believe in Him out of love and goodwill towards Him. He does not wish to force people into belief through incontrovertible evidence or irresistible arguments and therefore if people disbelieve, it is by an act of their own free will. That is not to say that God has not left convincing evidence and reasons for His existence—He obviously has—but such data is only available to those who want it and denied to those who wilfully close their minds, such as Google-Brain. The biblical sting in the tail, though, is contained in Psalm 14: *dixit insipiens in corde suo non est Deus* (the fool hath said in his heart, there is no God).

GOOD WITHOUT GOD?

I ponder: is there such a thing as "good without God," which is the universal position of most people nowadays? I have listened to many people who claim to be good and kind and yet do not believe in any God. They give money to charity, stay married faithfully until death, and help old ladies across the road. Although we have the natural law written in our hearts—a notion which Mr Google-Brain will no doubt deny, because it points to the existence of God—this law does become worn out or perhaps frayed at the edges. We all want to be good and that's fine. But supposing we are put to the test and have to choose between good and evil?

THE STORY OF BRIAN

A man works for an investment bank in London, let's call him Brian. Brian is a trader and a very successful one who earns a lot of money. He is happily married and sober, and has children. He spends time with his family and is generous to his friends. He regularly goes to church, even. There is only one problem, which is very common amongst wealthy people: he could really do with a tiny bit more money.

One morning he is at his desk on the bank's trading floor and has a "eureka" moment. By accident, he discovers that by twiddling a few keys and making a few minor adjustments he has credited his personal bank account with one hundred pounds. Having checked all the data he realises that this tiny sum of money (he deals in millions of pounds every day) has fallen through the system and cannot be traced by anyone. Brian makes no attempt to replace the money; he has no idea how to do this anyway. He goes home to his family and puts the whole incident behind him although he knows deep down that he has stolen from the bank. He really should have reported this to his manager and together they would attempt to replace the small sum but, well, life's too short and this wasn't worth the bother. Reporting the incident to the authorities may be a risky strategy anyway, not only because his honesty might be questioned, but also because his manager is a bit of a crook himself and would not appreciate Brian raising the issue.

The following month Brian receives an unexpected bill from his wine merchant which he can afford, obviously, but it will leave him a bit short as he was hoping to pay for an extra-special family holiday. His mind turns to the recent fiddle on his computer. Having wrestled with his conscience and won, he taps a few keys and, glory be, he can afford the wine bill and the holiday. So, everybody's happy and there is absolutely no way that he can be discovered. We can guess the rest of this story as Brian gets more and more greedy until, eventually, he ruins the bank.

Exactly what defences should Brian have had in place to fortify himself against such insidious temptations? Perhaps he was a genuinely honest person in his daily life and would never shortchange anyone. But temptations originate from the Devil, whether or not we believe in him, who knows our weaknesses intimately and in great detail. A simple belief in God, coupled with weekly visits to Mass, may not be enough to save Brian, I'm afraid. The only defence available to people in such circumstances is a deep love of God which, in turn, results in a hatred and fear of sin. Even the fear of offending God may not be sufficient, nor the prospect of eternal damnation which is also a possibility if indeed God exists. The only real protection against a fall in Brian's case is an awareness of God's presence and to be in love with Him. As I have said, *nothing else works*.

Assuming that such love is a rarity amongst humankind, it is terrifying to speculate how many people will succumb just like Brian.

WE ALL LIKE TO BE THANKED

Although Mr Google-Brain is full to the brim with human kindness and possesses massive helpings of natural virtue, being a nice chap will not keep him out of hell, if hell indeed exists. Being a splendid fellow is its own reward because we all feel good about being nice. It's nice when we are kind and people are nice and kind back. It feels good to donate one's surplus cash to charity—only the surplus, mind—and to help organise the annual fireworks party for disabled children. Of course, one expects to be rewarded for one's kindness with, perhaps, a letter of thanks or even a knighthood. Even when giving way to allow an oncoming vehicle to pass on a narrow lane entitles us to a cheery wave and, better still, a flash of the headlamps or, even better, a toot on the horn. Occasionally, I have been allowed to pass a stationary car on a lane and forget to wave cheerily or flash my lights or toot the horn. There is an angry explosion from the stationary driver who shakes his fist and yells through his driver's side window. Even William Shakespeare confirms this through the mouth of King Lear: "how sharper than a serpent's tooth it is to have a thankless child." We all recognise that Lear's rage was a little overdone for dramatic purposes, but the principle is still there: we all refuse to do something for nothing. Having described natural virtue, one cannot dismiss it as some kind of vice, far from it. Yet natural virtue is only a start when attempting to acquire supernatural virtue, which is essential if we wish to go to heaven. It is upon the bedrock of natural virtue that we build the true virtue which is pleasing to God. Supernatural virtue is doing something good for the greater glory of God and for the salvation of our own soul and the souls of others.

2010: OUR LORD IS BETRAYED

In the spring, the *Spectator* magazine in the UK stages a public debate in central London entitled, "This house expects England to be a Catholic Country," a laughable proposition in any language. The debate itself, which I attend, is informative and the chief features of it are, firstly, that the defenders of our religion are pathetically weak. One guest speaker, a bishop, claims that the Catholic Church is good because of all the money it raises for charity. Secondly, the anti-Catholic speakers are in full throttle. One of them, Matthew Parris, lampoons the Church in thoroughly Calvinistic terms as he denounces the sale of indulgences, the "hocus pocus" of the Mass, and the appallingly repressive rules on clerical celibacy. All good for a laugh and I am amused as it was clear that, in spite of attempts at modernisation, the Church is still regarded by its enemies as not having changed since the Middle Ages. If only!

At the conclusion of the formal speeches, the microphone is handed around to the audience for comments. I have my contribution ready but unfortunately I am not called upon to speak. Here is what I was going to say: "If God does not exist then Mr Parris is right to tear the Church to pieces. Indeed, one could go further and say that without God the Church is a worldwide criminal enterprise which takes money from the poor and gives it to the rich. The dictatorship of the clergy and their oppression of ordinary people is a scandal. On the other hand, if God *does* exist then those on the platform who speak in favour of the Church do Him less than justice. If there is an all-powerful, all-knowing and loving God above us, then everything changes. The idea of separation of Church and state would therefore be ridiculous because the state must naturally turn to God as its author and source of power. If God does exist, this means that the Bible is all true: the resurrection, the miracles... Nations must bend the knee to the deity and adjust all public and private life in accordance with His authority and precepts."

This was the absolute position of the Catholic Church up until the Second Vatican Council (1962–1965) and, like all the teachings of the Church, it is utterly logical and reasonable. One is forced to conclude that if you claim to believe in God but do not accept what that belief entails, then you are agnostic. Hardly anyone nowadays disputes the desirability of the separation of Church and state, even Catholics. Yet, if God exists, this position is nonsense. It is depressing how almost nobody is able or willing to stand up for the Church nowadays and one of the essential ingredients of a recovery is a modern-day St Edmund Campion. In the history of the Catholic Church, in all the ages we have seen clergy and laymen who were heroic in their defence of holy religion and able to use the powers of reason in order to make converts. The *Spectator* debate was so one-sided because those Catholics, who should have known better, were unable to defend themselves against the eloquent and forceful onslaught they faced. They simply have no grounding in apologetics and are obviously ignorant of basic theology.

2013: HOPES DASHED

The chief event this year is that we have a new pope, Pope Francis. One of my close friends has been praising Cardinal Bergoglio, as he is convinced that he is a traditional prelate who will proclaim the timeless teachings of the Church and put it back on its feet. My initial reaction to this is regret that things have now got so bad that the future and stability of the body of Christ depends on the personal opinions of the Holy Father. When I watch Pope Francis appearing on the balcony for the first time, and presented to the crowd in St Peter's Square, I inwardly groan at his first words: "Good evening!" Keeping the Catholic faith nowadays is harder than ever, with the growing debate amongst Catholics as to whether we have a valid Pope, as *sedevacantism* is becoming a boom industry. This debate, which occupies the pages of many current journals, has been fanned by the words and actions of our increasingly eccentric Holy Father, Pope Francis.

In entering a debate there is often a tendency to start off with your conclusion, through the exercise of the will or the emotions, and then to gradually work backwards to justify your position. The danger of this procedure, of which we are all guilty from time to time, is to disregard any evidence which challenges our preconceived notions. Our conclusion may even contradict such evidence. The use of *ad hominem* arguments is very common also, such as: "Well, someone like him *would* say that, wouldn't he?" The other obvious danger present in this line of thinking is that it can result in such an entrenched opinion that bitter strife ensues. One thing for sure is that the holder of views which have been acquired in this manner is unshakeable and impervious to alternative opinions, regarding any argument more in terms of a personal attack.

In most areas of human endeavour such attitudes may be completely harmless and part of the cut and thrust of real life. After all, who would want a world where everyone argued on the basis of incontrovertible evidence with no room for emotions of any kind? In addition, on any given issue, who is right? Access to objective truth in issues outside the perennial teaching of the Church might be beyond our means. That is why, presumably, hundreds of historians dispute the causes of the First World War, for example. All we can know for certain is that historians may all be wrong about a particular subject, but it is impossible that they can all be right.

SEDEVACANTISM IS LARGELY EMOTIONAL

There's a huge and emergent danger to the faith of good and loyal Catholics, and that is the proliferation of the *sedevacantist* (SV) position. I refer here to the theory that we have not had a Pope since the death of Pope Pius XII in 1958. There is a multiplicity of variations on that theme, such as Pope Francis is not the true pope because of the invalidity of his election, but I propose to stick with the authentic SV position which is that the See of Peter has been vacant since 1958. I do not do so for arbitrary reasons or for convenience. I do so because I do not believe that Pope Francis is any worse than his postconciliar predecessors. If Francis automatically relinquishes his throne because of heresy, then all the Popes since 1958 are equally guilty. The fact that some of them were not as bad as Francis doesn't acquit them of invalidity, according to the SV proponents. One has only to recall the appalling prayer meeting at Assisi (1986) to be reminded how Pope John Paul II did incalculable harm. And how about Pope Paul VI imposing a novel and un-Catholic rite of Mass on the unsuspecting faithful? That surely places him high on a pedestal in the rogues' gallery!

I have examined, so far as my poor brain is able, the theological arguments for, and against, the proposition that the See of Peter has been vacant since the death of Pope Pius XII and I have tentatively concluded that these arguments are finely balanced. One thing is for sure, though, and it is that one cannot be certain whether *any* of the theological authorities had reckoned with the postconciliar popes. There is really no precedent in Church history for the successor of Peter to announce that all religions lead to God, for example. The canonists and theologians, indeed some of the greatest minds in the Church nowadays, are really dealing with a new conundrum.

The greatest threat to the Catholic Church comes, not necessarily from the intellectual elite, but from ordinary Catholics who love their faith and are nursing in varying degrees a sense of being betrayed by the Holy See. They say, "He can't possibly be the Pope. Just listen to what he said on the plane last week!" I have also heard: "I gave up on the papacy when John Paul II kissed the Koran." I expect that the prayer meeting at Assisi must have bolstered the *sede* ranks. And what about putting Pachamama on the altar? And blessing homosexual couples? We are now faced with the huge problem that many Catholics take one look at the sovereign pontiff and say, "No thank you!" These are usually good people who cannot bear to witness the attacks on their beloved Church. Some of them may start to work backwards and read the excellent literature available on the internet, but in doing so, most will filter out all those arguments which proclaim that we still have a valid pope. Many have turned to SV websites. For Catholic content, all these outlets are irresistible: they instruct, and they entertain. Who can resist the almost salacious voyeurism of *Novus Ordo Watch* and the eloquent episcopal outrage of Bishop Sanborn? Both websites are masterful in their exposition of all that is wrong with the papacy and always end up by jeering at what they call the "recognise and resist" position.

PROMINENT SEDEVACANTISTS I HAVE KNOWN

I am drawn to some of the SV websites because in some ways they do a service to the Church by stating confidently and clearly where the Pope is going wrong. I do switch off, however, when the "recognise and resist" bit comes at the end. This is because, compared with their nightmare solution that we have no popes, I much prefer muddling through the crisis and learning about how to defend my Catholic faith whilst taking every announcement from the papal throne with a huge pinch of salt. "Aha!," they reply, "by picking and choosing which part of the Pope's teaching you prefer, you are no better than a Protestant!" I am so used to this line of argument that, not finding an answer, I have been momentarily persuaded by it. I began to think that, after all, perhaps I *am* a Protestant! Yet I know, along with all those other "recognise and resist" Catholics, that I am trying to do my best in the face of a dire situation which has never existed before in the history of the Church. However, faithful to the Holy See I shall remain because I know, from the bottom of my heart, that of all the sins I commit during my life, attachment to the Holy See is not one of them and God will not punish me for refusing the SV position. We have to hold onto our trust and confidence that God will put everything right in His own time. It is not for us mere mortals to try to do it for ourselves.

For the vast majority of laymen and clergy who have abandoned the Pope in favour of the various versions of sedevacantism, it doesn't end there. In the spiritual life one gets better or one gets worse. One doesn't simply stay the same. From initially laughing at the Holy Father and mocking his Indian headdress, one can graduate to open and vehement dislike, aided and abetted by the internet. It will not be long before one goes only to SV Masses, which may not happen more than once a month in special chapels where prayers for the Pope are left out. Sermons designed to fortify the faithful in the SV position can ultimately wear them down and they may start to miss Mass altogether as despair takes hold. Finally, they may give up their Catholic religion, which was what the Devil was planning all along.

ALL IN GOD'S HANDS

It is the duty of every Catholic to pray for the Holy Father and do penance for him, however ghastly we think he is. I do not rule out the possibility that we have not had a valid Pope since Pius XII, as it is a theory one can expound in the lounge bar. However, this view is definitely not demanded by the Catholic faith and, as St Paul advises us in the epistle for the Third Sunday of Advent: *Nihil solliciti sitis: sed in omni oratione*... translated roughly "stop worrying and start praying"! At the general judgment we will know the answers to all these questions, but it is not for us to abandon hope and the salvation upon which it depends. In the current era of Catholic history, where so much has been taken away from us—the Mass, Catholic teaching, and Catholic morality, to name a few—we have to hold on to what God has left us, by our fingernails if need be. As Sebastian Flyte exclaims in *Brideshead Revisited*: "It's so hard being a Catholic!"

CHAPTER 12

How to Protect Children

OUR CHILDREN AND THE INTERNET

In his tireless campaign to disrupt the peace of families, Satan has today hit upon something incredibly powerful: the universal availability of the internet.

It was television which heralded the start of family disunity, and a few Catholic parents regarded it (correctly in my view) as so divisive and corrupting that they banned it from the family home. After all, if dad insists on watching hours of baseball, what kind of example is that to his children who, quite reasonably, want to watch their own entertainment? Quite often, if TV was banned in a family home, the kids would promptly trot down to a friend's house and watch it there, precipitating hour upon hour of absenteeism from family life, or rather, what was left of it.

Although we managed to ban the TV, my wife and I were very fortunate in that we managed to bring up our ten children in the days before the scourge of the internet. It was also fortunate that we lived originally in remote countryside so there were no neighbours upon whom our children could rely for their TV watching. This was during the era of bulky desktop computers and before the arrival of broadband, thus access to the web was preceded by a grinding and whistling noise and the slow arrival of the information which one sought. Mobile telephones were just that, telephones, and phone calls were the most popular methods of communication.

Computers were already posing a threat to parental authority over children in the guise of electronic games. These universally gripped the imagination of many youngsters so that the "secret garden" mentality began to take hold. The secret garden mentality was formed when children withdrew from family life and entered into the artificial and enticing world of "Space Invaders," racing cars, and the rest. There were hundreds of games to choose from, and children would wear themselves out as they stared at the screen for hours, often long into the night if they were able. In those days it was unusual for children to have their own computers, so parents were able to bargain with their offspring in this way: "If you do your homework we will allow you an hour on the computer." Such arrangements became burdensome for mum and dad because the computer had such a hold over their children that they often found they had to give way to increased demands. Not to do so might, and often did, appear unreasonable. Before the wholesale graduation to the internet, it was still possible for children to pass their time playing games which were not so innocent as Space Invaders. I recall visiting a family in town and being shown into their young son's bedroom. A group of boys were sitting on a bed looking at a large screen and holding remote controls. The game consisted of a lone gunman shooting up staff and patients in a make-believe hospital. The graphics were so realistic as to show blood splatter.

The advent of handheld computer devices has now utterly overturned the lives of children and has presented parents with an insoluble problem. The appeal to children's curiosity of being able to access the internet on their smartphones is overpowering. The worst kind of filth is available at the click of a button, and this is a huge temptation for everyone, especially children, who have become more and more reliant on their phones. It is almost impossible for parents to control their children's activities on the internet and, consequently, authority in families becomes disrupted. All family members are welded to their mobile phones and one can often see, when visiting a household, that everyone is clutching a device as they check for messages, send and receive social media communications, watch the news headlines or do their shopping. When the children are alone, one can only guess at what they are getting up to in the privacy of their bedrooms.

... AND THE ANSWER?

So, what on earth can parents do to stem the tide and restore family life? Generally speaking, once children lose their innocence and become addicted to pornography, there is little one can do to reverse the situation. The attachment to vice, once established, often makes it impossible to "unring the doorbell"; innocence lost is almost impossible to recover. Internet pornography is at the centre of the crisis amongst youngsters as it is so readily available. Various solutions have been attempted by parents, but they are hamstrung by the fact that mum and dad are also habitually online, and maybe dad is just as addicted to pornography as his offspring. This is a fact, and even for those parents who are practising their Catholic faith, it is almost impossible to break free in spite of regular recourse to the confessional.

I have often heard parents of very young children, aware of the likely problems they may face in the future, assure themselves that they will not allow their kids to have smartphones until they become young adults. While this is admirable, it is a general fact of life that you cannot protect someone from himself. If a child is determined to enter into the world of vice, then, ultimately, nothing can stop him.

The modern crisis surrounding the internet is yet another stage in the attack on families and society which is organised by the Devil. It leads not only to the damnation of countless individuals but also to the destruction of families, resulting in the dissolution of Christian society. Like every major crisis, it has at its root a supernatural cause, and it can thus be overcome only through supernatural means. Fear of hell and fear of God help but are not a reliable motivation to protect people from this most powerful and dangerous element in modern life—the internet. Fear of a good telling off by the priest in confessional can achieve limited results, but how many people who sin in this way avoid going to confession to Father "Nasty" and watch with relief as Father "Nice" enters the confessional box?

If this cat and mouse game with one's vices continues for any length of time, there is a risk of eventually "making peace with one's sin." This is a disaster and may well lead to abandonment of the Catholic faith, allowing despair to take root.

The question is: how can one overcome sin and remain in a state of grace? The answer is to replace fear of God with love of God because we are far less likely to offend someone we love. I am not talking about a kind of "happy clappy" love where God is regarded as a being who loves us however much we insult Him. No, we have to go further and be "in love" with God. This "love" achieves a union with Christ, and it is something we have to pray for as it is a great gift of grace which we cannot achieve on our own. Children often find it easier to be in love with God as they have an inbuilt innocence which grace can animate. Adults find that being in love with God is harder because it involves great humility to acknowledge that He is everything and we are nothing.

Parents must ensure that they set a good example to their children as a first step in their quest to instil devotion amongst their offspring. The huge prize which results from this is the development of holy innocence, where the children shun any temptation to offend God. Daily family rosary is a marvellous weapon in the battle against temptation but, first of all, mum and dad must, absolutely must, try to pray on their own before the children come down to breakfast. If they do this, it is unlikely that they will ever have to force their children to attend family rosary. In every family the parents have to kneel down on their own and pray earnestly for God to enter the hearts of their offspring. I know this may sound extreme, but the problems faced by modern families are now so ghastly that they demand serious and regular prayer.

God will provide the answer to this powerful and dangerous threat to families. He will ensure that the children remain innocent. It is only innocence that will make a child flee for his life from evil influences, having developed a healthy horror of sin.

Our children's schools, especially the boys' school, were hot on the track of temptations to impurity by their charges. Every boy had a priest confessor throughout those difficult teenage years, one who took a keen interest in their moral development. Mobile phones were banned (although this was before the arrival of the smartphone) and there was no access to television. So, although Camblain-l'Abbé priests made the boys into men, they also encouraged a purity which was almost childlike.

SCHOOLING FOR OUR CHILDREN

Children, given the right encouragement, will always take to the Latin Mass, as they are struck by its beauty and solemnity. They may even willingly join in family prayers and other devotions. Encouraging as all this is, the future will always be uncertain as they come across the counterculture in the form of non-Catholic friends and other alien influences.

We were fortunate enough to be able to send our offspring to traditional Catholic schools in France, but most people are certainly not in a position to do this through lack of finances, living too far away, or both. I should add that, if mum and dad are not switched on to the life of grace and the necessary striving for perfection, it may be useless sending them to France. This is because the schools insist upon the convergence of their priorities with those of the parents. Quite often, I have witnessed lukewarm mums and dads who go through the hugely expensive and inconvenient ordeal of sending their children abroad, only to continue to provide at home a culture and an atmosphere which is contrary to the Catholic life. This manifests itself when there arises some problem or other at the school, where mum and dad either side with their child against the school authorities or, even worse, try to be even-handed and act as a kind of referee between the school and the child. I have often heard some parents inflict sharp criticism on the teachers, and even in the hearing of their offspring. Such attitudes run the risk of setting all the benefits of a truly Catholic education at nought. On one occasion, I heard a daughter, who was being educated by the Dominicans, poke fun at her teacher nun in front of her dad. He responded: "Silly nuns!" In cases such as this, it is quite likely that the child will feel insecure at school and there is much evidence that, ultimately, she may abandon her religion completely.

In our own case, we have frequently received complaints about our children from both schools in France. This is because they aren't saints by any means. We have always reacted by firmly taking the school's side rather than that of our children. Even in the case of rank unfairness, the principle is the same. The maxim "injustice is preferable to disorder" is so true.

For most parents, for whom the French schools are an impossibility, the question remains as to how to educate their children. An obvious answer lies in the provision of homeschooling. Even as I write, however, the knives are being sharpened by the government to close off this option or, at least, make it so difficult as to render it impractical. In any case, homeschooling, although invaluable for youngsters, is not recommended for children over the age of, say, twelve years. Human beings are social animals and, in time, children will pine for the company of friends. Homeschool co-ops and hybrid models are a good way to meet this need.

STATE SCHOOLS AN OPTION?

The only option available to many parents is state schools, private schools being prohibitively expensive. There is a common feeling amongst Catholic parents that state schools, especially comprehensives,[1] are more like cesspits. We have all gained this impression by hearing anecdotes about drug abuse, bullying, and other generally appalling behaviour by the pupils. It must be admitted that such schools are far from ideal, especially with the imposition of the national curriculum, which accepts sexual deviancy as normal. Comprehensive schools do differ vastly in quality, however, and if parents are considering

---

1 A "comprehensive school" is a state-funded secondary school which does not select its pupils on the basis of academic achievement or aptitude; any pupil can attend, irrespective of social class or ability, and they are all taught together. Such schools usually serve pupils from the age of 11 to the ages of 16 or 18.

one of these, it may be sensible to examine in detail the quality of schools which claim to be "Catholic." The presentation of the new, post-Vatican-II religion may confuse a child to such an extent that he may find it hard to reconcile the contradictions between school and home. It may be better if the child is sent to a nondenominational establishment where the Catholic Faith is not under direct attack. Above all, the best action is for parents to move heaven and earth to ensure that their children receive the milk and honey of a traditional Catholic education.

Supported by the solid prayer life of the parents, God will protect their children from corruption, even in a comprehensive school. But they must assist God by not deliberately and knowingly exposing their children to danger. In a nondenominational school, it is perfectly possible, but by no means easy, for the children to maintain their Catholicism. Indeed, given the waywardness of most of the other pupils, frequently coming as they do from backgrounds of broken homes, often addicted to smartphones and other modern miseries, truly Catholic children may offer these other kids some hope. It is quite reasonable, therefore, to assert that, provided the home life of one's children is impregnated with a love of God and His Church, and provided that the parents take no unjustifiable risks with Catholic state schools, their children will maintain their faith. I have seen this with my own eyes. Likewise, if the family life is not right, then even the best Catholic schools in France will have little effect on them. There is plenty of evidence of this, also. The sanctification of our youngsters is always the work of Divine Providence and parents are a merely a conduit for the flow of grace. So long as mum and dad do not actually block the flow of grace by taking unjustified risks, they can rely on Our Lady to protect their offspring. This great grace will be granted, always, but only if it is begged for on a daily basis.

THE HEAVY LIFTING

In order to sanctify family life, it is not sufficient for mum and dad to make the little ones kneel down and recite the rosary. We all know how chaotic family rosary can be! Taking them to Mass and keeping them quiet in church is also a burdensome task. Educating them in the Faith and reading them the lives of the saints is also worthwhile, but none of this is enough. Get up early and say an extra decade of the rosary before the children get up! In the life of a family there is so much to pray for, and it is this heavy lifting which will invite divine intervention on such a massive scale so that a project which starts off facing major problems can instead reap huge blessings.

"Sufficient unto the day is the evil thereof." These words from Our Lord's Sermon on the Mount must form the concrete foundation of family life, and in particular, decisions about schooling. Parents have to ascertain the will of God through their prayer and sacrifice. The divine will is always manifested in such a way that all doubts and worries about what the future holds are dispelled, and the obvious course of action in a particular matter is the only one left. I am not suggesting that we treat God as some kind of Father Christmas; we have to show a deep love for Him and accept His authority over our lives, even if the result may not be to our liking. Clare and I gave up a beautiful farm in the heart of the countryside, we had to say goodbye to our cow and all the other animals. We had to move to the other side of the country in order to facilitate the attendance of our children at French schools. Our life for the following twenty years involved long and arduous journeys in our minibus, ferrying children all over France. And the result? God has preserved the Catholic Faith in our offspring and called two of our boys to the priesthood and one daughter to the religious life. Our other children have embarked on splendid Catholic marriages, producing, at the last count, eighteen grandchildren, with three more on the way, so far.

"As arrows are in the hand of a mighty man; so are children of the youth. Happy is the man that hath his quiver full of them: they shall not be ashamed, but they shall speak with the enemies in the gate" (Psalm 126:4).

CHAPTER 13

First Fruits

2015: NEW HOUSE

We are now living in Salisbury Road, Dover. Clare and I are alone, as all our children have flown the nest. Just before our youngest, Josephine, left her French school, God took away our house in Guise. To be more precise, it was requisitioned by the administrators of my business, which had gone bust. This house was an asset of my limited company for various tax reasons, which had been explained to me by my accountant at the time. Our original house in Park Avenue, Dover, was sold off and the mortgage settled, and Salisbury Road is rented to us by Clare's niece.

Right now, we own nothing, and we owe nothing. I have to admit that the absence of credit cards and a mortgage is a truly liberating feeling. If we have nothing in the bank, we eat sorrel soup from the garden. I am referred to by a few friends, not as Job on his dunghill, but as Joe on his dunghill. And yet we are far more fortunate than Job as we are able to live, albeit carefully and frugally. Our new house is far from a dunghill, with plenty of room and a beautiful garden in which we grow fruits and vegetables.

Clare has a new job, which is part time, and thankfully it is a source of great satisfaction to her. She works as an independent advocate, employed to support those unfortunate souls who lack mental capacity and have no one to support them. On three days a week she visits these people in their residential homes or in hospital, where they are confined for their own and the public's protection. Many of them are seriously handicapped by being nonverbal. Often, they are incarcerated through drink or drug abuse and have often been abandoned by their relatives.

VISITORS

I have always made a point of being on good terms with priests in our diocese of Southwark and they are always welcome in our house. When we lived in Somerset, we lost touch with the diocesan clergy because, not only were they a rarity, but we lived in seclusion as we inhabited a remote part of the countryside. In those days we hardly ever met a diocesan priest and were content with the ministrations of the two traditional priests we knew, Father Lessiter and Father Crowdy. Once we moved to Dover, however, a friend of ours, who was a pillar of the local Novus Ordo parish, aware as he was of our commitment to Catholic Tradition, took it upon himself to work for our "reconversion" to the modern Church. In the early months after our arrival at the seaside town, we were introduced to the local parish priest and some of his priestly assistants. We got on with them extremely well and they made no attempts to "reconvert" us. In actual fact, in their company over frequent dinners, barbecues, and other social events, the subject of religion never seemed to come up. Most of them asked us for money, though!

As we settled in our new town, we also made friends with several local clergy who were offering the Traditional Latin Mass in various parishes in the vicinity, thanks largely to the loosening of the restrictions by Pope Benedict XVI. Most of these priests were of above-average intelligence compared with those whom we had met previously, and they all exhibited a very touching love of the Old Mass, which they would say as often as possible. Occasionally they would say Mass for us in our little basement chapel. I took the view that I should support and encourage these priests as much as possible and yet, charming as they were, I was never able to tease out of them why they felt able to continue to say the Novus Ordo Mass. The only admission which they made was that they were "uncomfortable" with the New Mass but would not elucidate. I would not impute dishonourable motives to anyone, least of all priests who are "biritual," as it is termed, yet a cynic might suggest that they are terrified of losing preferment in the Church and would rather not upset the local bishop. I know of only two priests in our diocese who refuse to say the New Mass, one of whom is living the life of a hermit in a remote cottage, and the other is languishing in Rome. The bishop refuses to employ them despite the chronic shortage of active clergy.

Ever since the reform of Catholic seminaries after Vatican II, the seminarians have been denied the true theology of the Mass. Rather, much emphasis has been placed on the role of the priest as the "leader of the people of God" and "president of the assembly." In addition, I know for a fact that in modern seminaries, the students are farmed out to parishes for at least half of the six years at college to do "pastoral and outreach work." All this is well and good; however, the risk arises that these newly ordained priests enter their new parishes with massive projects in mind, often wanting to turn things upside down and carry out "initiatives." I think that most of their seminary training concentrates on techniques designed to attract back to church those millions of souls who have, for various reasons, abandoned ship. The training in such activities (let us call them "gimmicks") is not what a seminary is for.

The priestly training my two sons received in the Society of St Pius X is miles beyond that of modern seminaries, as they are given a firm grounding in spirituality and philosophy. I was at school with a boy who was very pious and went into seminary. He emerged bristling with new ideas and initiatives which he proceeded to activate in his first parish, as a curate. Thanks to the resistance of a rather crusty parish priest, and the lethargy of his flock, he despaired so deeply that he left the ministry and married a teacher at the local Catholic school. One has only to read the life of Saint John Vianney, the Curé d'Ars, to realise that the life of a priest is primarily one of prayer and sacrifice. When this saint arrived at his new parish during the eighteenth century, he found a dilapidated church with a few old ladies in his congregation. There is a description of the immorality amongst the population which extended to "lewd" public dances! Upon observing this, rather than activate "pastoral initiatives" and "outreach," he simply fasted on cold potatoes and lived a life of prayer and, of course, his daily Mass. In a short time, the French authorities were forced to build a special railway station at Ars to accommodate the thousands of visitors to the Curé's Mass. The Devil was not well pleased and, in desperation, set fire to the priest's bed with him still lying in it. "If there were two more priests like you in France, my kingdom would be over!" That is what the Devil said to him. I have visited the famous church at Ars and can report that the Latin Mass, so beloved by the saint, has been banned!

If these poor priests straight out of seminary are not already completely discouraged by the realities of parish life, some of them then discover the Tridentine Mass. If they start saying this Mass on a regular basis, one of two things may follow: either the congregation complains to the bishop who comes down hard upon the priest or, worse still, he discovers where the true heart and soul of his priesthood lies and has a panic attack. This often leads to the priest making peace with two contradictory sides to his religion, and he carries on with the New Mass because he is fearful that he doesn't really have a priestly vocation which would withstand the doctrinal, intellectual, and spiritual rigours of the Tridentine Mass. I have seen priests fall by the wayside soon after discovering the Old Mass and falling in love with it.

There is no doubt that all the diocesan priests I have met who know the Traditional Latin Mass are "in love" with it. They all, with the two heroic exceptions I mentioned, also say the Novus Ordo Mass regularly in their parishes. They are unwilling to abandon the Novus Ordo, however, because the New Mass has become their default position, it being the only recognisable link with their priestly training. I have a feeling, judging by their reluctance to discuss the matter with me (perhaps because they regard it as none of my business), that should they abandon the New Mass completely, their entire world would collapse around their ears.

2018: VOCATION

My wife and I are walking from our house towards Dover beach along with Bridget, our eldest daughter, who is on a short visit. As we approach the sea front, Bridget says:

"I've got something to tell you."

We stop walking and stare at her quizzically.

"I've made a decision," she continues. "I've been accepted as a postulant by the Dominican convent in St. Pré."

I am reminded of a similar conversation which occurred some years back when one of our previous au pairs, Theresa, paid us a visit. She was from a large Catholic family, similar to ours, and had also attended the Dominican nuns' school in France. We had not heard from Theresa for quite some time and our last intelligence was that she might have a boyfriend. One day, she telephoned us to ask if she could come to stay as she wanted to hitch a lift to France. As we were still travelling to our French house every fortnight, we were happy to agree. I remember saying to Clare something along the lines that, perhaps we shouldn't mention anything about religion to Theresa when she visited, as she might have given up all that. When she appeared at our front door, the ex-au pair was dressed in a leather jacket and denim jeans. I immediately thought that my suggestion to Clare was justified.

"I have a small announcement," she said a little later, over tea. (Uh-oh, we thought. Pregnant perhaps?)

"I've been accepted by the Carmelites in Belgium!"

Bridget, unknown to us, had also tried the same Carmel in Quievrain but they had turned her down. The life of the traditional Carmelite nun is very hard indeed and not for the faint-hearted. They are completely enclosed and are not allowed to see anyone except their nearest relatives. Other visitors may speak with the nuns but not actually see them as they hide around the corner out of sight. At Mass in the convent chapel, which we visited occasionally, the nuns are completely invisible, as they are positioned, during Mass, to the left of the high altar and behind a huge iron grille. We can, of course, hear their beautiful singing.

Whereas most "official" monasteries or convents are amalgamating and often closing down due to the lack of vocations, the "rebel" (traditional) houses are thriving, and every year sees the arrival of increasing numbers of young people willing and able to serve God by giving their lives to him. The Carmel in Quievrain has recently opened a daughter house in the United States, where Theresa is now mistress of novices.

We never had Bridget marked down as a future nun, far from it! After leaving the Dominican convent school in Le Herie, she studied in Paris and gained her degree. Like most young ladies in that city, she seemed to be a bit of a barfly. She once took me to *Le Dernier Metro* which was near the Eiffel Tower, and she seemed to know everybody in the bar. On our visits to Paris, Clare and I would attend Sunday Mass at Saint-Nicolas du Chardonnet, near the River Seine. I have to say that attendance at this church, which had been forcibly occupied by the faithful of the Society of St Pius X many years back, was like being at Kings Cross station during the rush hour. As one Mass ended and another started, there would be a huge surge of people, including young men in their fashionable pink trousers, in and out of the building. There was a lot of Catholic action which centred on "St Nic's," as they called it, including special Masses and instruction for university students. For a time, Bridget sang in the church choir, as did many of her friends. The traditional youth group attached to the church was very active and apostolic as they made huge efforts to convert their lapsed and non-Catholic friends to the Faith—a practice which some postconciliar popes seem to condemn, especially Pope Francis!

The French experience underlines an important point, which I have frequently made: for the young to remain steadfast in their religion, it may not be enough for them to follow mum and dad. It is essential that they have friends of their own age who share the Faith. With the great numbers of traditional Catholic communities in Paris, to be a "traddy" is regarded as "cool."

Bridget had a nice young man in tow (several, actually), and this particular chap, who was hoping to get serious, had to be told that she was joining a convent. So, what started out as a romantic date ended up as a rather solemn farewell. Poor man! He took it very well, though. Another lesson which we learned was that God calls people from all backgrounds and ways of life. Young people who join religious orders, as well as seminarians, are often the most unlikely specimens, according to us at any rate. But God sees things which we cannot fathom. All He requires is a generous heart and He will do the rest. One famous saint, St John Bosco, once claimed that one in three young people has a vocation. It is a pity that the world, with its pressures to conform, forces so many to ignore the call.

Bridget's announcement engenders mixed feelings. As we absorb its magnitude we are in a state of some shock; it was the last thing we were expecting. After we return to the house at the end of our walk, Bridget describes how she had been thinking about a vocation for a few years and how she had tried applying to the Carmel. We had no inkling that she was planning this.

In the time leading up to her departure, Bridget gives away most of her clothes and other possessions. This adds to our heartache as it reminds us that she will never return home, ever. Finally, the day of departure arrives in the early autumn, we pack her suitcase into the car, and set off on our journey to

St. Pré, which is in the south of France. After a long drive we finally enter through the wrought iron gates of the Dominican mother house and, as we emerge from the car, are greeted by a group of happy and excited young nuns who make us very welcome. The convent is a beautiful château surrounded by lawns, a wooded area, and vegetable gardens. A little stream runs through the grounds. A new and large chapel is nearing completion and there are other modern buildings attached, including a large school hall. The mother house also operates as a girl's school and there are several other schools, which the nuns operate, dotted all over France.

We are introduced to many of the nuns, including the mistress of novices, who will supervise our daughter for two years. We visit the convent at least twice a year and exchange regular letters. Despite the fact that Bridget is happy and settled, I still feel a slight lump in my throat if I go into her old bedroom for some reason. Some of her belongings, such as books and CDs, still lie about and I have to remind myself that she has a new home, and it isn't in Dover.

As she becomes more settled, in her letters Bridget describes her life at the convent. Initially, she is asked to help in the kitchen and carelessly injures her hand with a knife whilst hurriedly slicing bread for the nuns' breakfast. As she attends to her bleeding hand, the pan of hot chocolate boils over and in a panic, she grasps the pan which is very hot. She promptly drops all the contents onto the kitchen floor. Fortunately, some other nuns enter the room wondering, no doubt, why their breakfast has not arrived, and are greeted by the grisly spectacle of Bridget covered in blood and chocolate. They are, of course, very kind and suggest that their new postulant should go and clean up whilst they take charge of the preparations. Bridget's other job is to make sure that the lights in the chapel are switched on and off at the correct time. So, she ends up switching off the lights at the wrong time and the whole community at prayer gets plunged into darkness. Our daughter is also put in charge of a section of the vegetable patch, and this gives her much joy and satisfaction as she discovers that, owing to the warm climate, all the tomatoes and courgettes grow to almost double the size of those she was used to in England.

Although we miss Bridget horribly, there are great blessings to be had with her in the convent, and the greatest of these is the knowledge that she is praying for us. When you know that someone is praying for you constantly, it makes you secure in the knowledge that you have a special heavenly protection, which is very encouraging. It is so simple for monks and nuns, she explained to me once, because as Catholics, we are often uncertain what the will of God is from time to time. Not so for them because God's will is contained in the monastic rule which they live by.

When we visit our daughter, we stay at the convent, joining in with the offices which they pray several times a day in the chapel. I am always struck by the happy atmosphere there. On one occasion, when Clare and I are having lunch in the visitors' dining room, we hear the sounds of merriment from the nuns' refectory close by. As we listen, they suddenly break into gales of laughter, the sound which echoes all over the building.

POPE FRANCIS

We are all bothered by the sight of Pope Francis running up the white flag when it comes to Catholic faith and morals. It seems that he is motivated by the twin evils of our age: desire for acceptance and fear of unpopularity. I often wonder what would happen if the Holy Father restated some salient items of Catholic dogma? First of all, I am thinking about this dogma: *extra Ecclesiam nulla salus*. This is defined as follows: "We declare, say, define, and pronounce that it is absolutely necessary for the salvation of every human creature to be subject to the Roman Pontiff."[1] If Pope Francis repeated this, one can only guess at what might happen. At the very least he would utterly destroy sixty years of ecumenical dialogue and cause a massive internal rift within the Catholic Church. He may even have to go into hiding! Yet it is the *extra Ecclesiam* dogma which has been at the heart of the Church's missionary activity for two thousand years and has been the overriding principle which animated most of the martyrs, some of whom were prepared to die horribly in its defence. Nowadays, very few Catholics would even dream of proposing this "outdated" notion. They would either deny it or qualify it out of existence, which is probably their preferred option. However, to do so does not

---

1 Pope Boniface VIII, the Bull *Unam Sanctam*, 1302.

remove this stumbling block in Church teaching, it merely attempts to bury it in a shallow grave, where it is at risk of springing back up to haunt us. It must resurrect itself in all its glory because it is the one reason for conversion to the Catholic Faith. Otherwise, why bother to be a Catholic at all?

Another shocking reality of recent Vatican teaching is outright condemnation of any attempt to convert someone—to proselytise—by several modern popes. Indeed, Pope Francis himself said that "the Church grows by our witness, in words and deeds—rather than through proselytization."[2]

THE ATTACK ON APOLOGETICS

The study of apologetics is the starting point of any "proselytization" because apologetics sets out the utter reasonableness of the Catholic Faith. Catholic apologetics is now discarded in favour of the vague recommendations by Pope Francis for "witness in words and deeds." Underlying traditional Church teaching is the notion that the Catholic Church is universal in time and space, and *everyone* has to convert to it in order to obtain salvation. You *have* to be Catholic! Oh dear! How inconvenient! This is impossible to proclaim nowadays without being regarded as a hate criminal, so no wonder the postconciliar popes have remained silent. How could they possibly speak out? Nowadays we have become used to Catholic clergy and senior laymen who correctly state the Church's teaching on, say, gay marriage, and yet hastily add that one does not have to be Catholic.

---

2 Address to Catechists, April 27, 2013.

Turning now to another area of Church teaching: sodomy is a sin crying out to heaven for vengeance. Imagine if the Holy Father restated *that*? Another hate crime! Worse than going into hiding, he would be locked up and they would throw away the key. So, what do the Church leaders say? Simply this: that homosexuals are acceptable for priestly training so long as they are not "active." But we all know, do we not, that impure thoughts or desires, if lingered over and savoured, are sinful and can eventually lead to sinful activity. In any case, if a man with homosexual tendencies is interviewed by the seminary rector, why on earth would he admit to such tendencies unless he was planning to act on them or had already done so? In order to comply with pro-LGBT legislation, the Church may well end up abolishing the sin of sodomy and I cannot see a way around it, as it is only a matter of time before an active homosexual is refused admission to a seminary, takes legal action, and wins his case. This will signal a total collapse of Catholic moral teaching, unless the Catholic hierarchy are prepared to go to jail having spoken up for the truth.

Another dogma of the Church is that Jesus Christ is King. This means that he has dominion not only over our hearts and minds, but also over nations and governments. We are so accustomed nowadays to the separation of Church and state that this essential part of Church teaching is, again, either ignored, sidelined, or qualified out of existence. A few years ago, my children and I visited the site of the martyrdom of St Thomas Becket in Canterbury cathedral. As we whispered a few intercessions to this great defender of the freedom of the Catholic Church from state interference by Henry II, a cathedral canon sidled up to us and announced in solemn tones: "That's what you get when you combine Church and state!"

Separation of Church and state should be an anathema to the true secular and spiritual order, so again, in common with *extra ecclesiam nulla salus* and the LGBT problem, the notion of the Kingship of Christ turns around and bites us. Having accepted the separation of Church and state, the state is now having to invent its own morality, which is being translated into oppressive laws. The interference by governments in the moral life of their citizens, previously a province of the Church, is now so commonplace that few people even bat an eyelid. The raft of measures which promote LGBT rights are a compelling example of this topsy-turvy intrusion into the social reign of Jesus Christ by politicians. And to complete this inversion, the post-Vatican II Church is adopting the secular values of governments, such as climate change, social justice, and religious freedom. Can we imagine what would happen if the Pope restated the doctrine of the social reign of Jesus Christ?

THE TRADITIONAL LATIN MASS IS UNDER THREAT

The proclamation of some Catholic doctrines would invite jail sentences of varying lengths, and so parts of Catholic life also become subject to alteration, in order to synchronize with public opinion, which holds that all religions are equally valid. This popular notion also has the Church authorities running scared and is the basis of the current attacks on the Latin Mass. Imagine if they compulsorily reinstated this Mass? That is an impossibility because it would give to the Church a uniqueness and a physical identity totally contrary to the spirit of the modern world. We are now witnessing an attack even on those Catholics who simply "like" the Latin Mass and are prepared to go along with the new orientations. No, its enemies have to *crush* this Mass, and that is what the Holy Father is hoping to do by lampooning its adherents in his memoir, called (without apparent ironic intention) *Hope*.

Whilst the Holy Father promotes secular values, he knows that he is secure, as the sedevacantist movement is not a significant threat to him. On the other hand, were he to restate Catholic doctrine in its eternal purity, there is little doubt that his position would be tenuous at the very least, as most of the bishops and faithful would probably abandon him. The question is: are there any amongst the Catholic hierarchy who are prepared to suffer for the Faith, like St Thomas Becket, in the face of overwhelmingly hostile governments, which are merely reflecting public opinion? It seems not. We can only hope and pray that God Himself sorts this problem out, perhaps by sending us another St Teresa of Avila. From a purely human point of view, this crisis is insoluble, requiring divine intervention which we must ask for on a daily basis by clinging to our rosaries.

THE DESTRUCTION OF MONASTICISM

I am talking to one of my many sisters over the telephone.

"How is Bridget?," she inquires.

"We visited her recently at the convent and she is very happy and settled," I reply.

After a little pause, my sister says: "Is she? I mean, is she *really*? Doesn't she miss you all?"

This is the common reaction of most people who cannot understand how it is that a pretty and intelligent young woman, such as our daughter, could shut herself away from the world and shun the prospect of marriage and children. There is an assumption that most nuns are, deep down, unhappy and if only they would visit a psychologist, he would be able to remove all the layers of self-deception and expose the "real" person underneath.

Dr. William Coulson was a disciple of the influential American psychologist Carl Rogers, and for many years a copractitioner of the latter's "nondirective" therapy. In 1964 he became chief of staff at Rogers' Western Behavioural Sciences Institute in California, where, he says, as the resident Catholic it became his task to "gather a cadre of facilitators to invade the Immaculate Heart of Mary community" of nuns, and later some two dozen other orders, among them the Sisters of Mercy, the Sisters of Providence, and the Jesuits. This was in response to an invitation from certain Catholic diocesan bishops. It was only in 1971 that he began to "back away" from his belief in psychotherapy, when its destructive effects on the religious orders—and on the Church and society in general—became apparent to him. Having abandoned his once-lucrative practice, Dr. Coulson now devotes his life to lecturing to Catholic and Protestant groups on the dangers of psychotherapy.

It's all very simple. If you do not believe in original sin, then you assume that, deep down and buried underneath all our "conditioning," there is basically a good person. In my own case I know that, deep down, I have all kinds of "issues" which I would prefer to keep buried and not discuss. That doesn't mean these issues go away, far from it. Let us imagine that in my deepest sleep I dream of murdering my father. Sigmund Freud would immediately identify within myself a "deep psychological need" which, if true, would be frightening indeed! If an experienced psychotherapist tied me to his couch, it wouldn't be very long before he would expose my own deepest thoughts and desires, including murdering my father and changing my wife! But all he has done is to uncover my original sin, which I have spent my life trying to drown out through a life of prayer, sacrifice, and reception of the sacraments. Contrary to so-called expert opinion, I am not finding "the real me." I am uncovering the natural propensity towards evil with which I was born and which will remain with me until my dying day. The "real me" only exists in so far as I am united to Jesus Christ and the Church which He founded. That is the true reality. My deep-down propensity towards evil has to be smothered by being in, and remaining in, a state of grace.

I mention Dr Coulson because he was one of the first psychologists to come to the conclusion that most psychotherapy is destructively evil and has huge unforeseen consequences. Who would have thought that the result of his project would be the utter destruction of the religious orders in the United States? Here is Dr Coulson in his own words: "It works, you know; one tumbles pretty easily into this. We corrupted a whole raft of religious orders on the west coast in the '60s by getting the nuns and priests to talk about their distress. The Institute of the Immaculate Heart of Mary had some sixty schools when we started; at the end, they had one. There were some 615 nuns when we began. Within a year after our first interventions, three hundred of them were petitioning Rome to get out of their vows. They did not want to be under anyone's authority, except the authority of their imperial inner selves."[3]

Much of the interview is unprintable as it describes the descent of many of the nuns into unspeakable vice. Modern doctors of the mind are almost universal in their opinion that suppressing one's "inner self" is *bad*, whereas "letting it all hang out," as they say, is *good*. They claim that, by releasing all the *bad*, one finds the innate *good* somehow lurking underneath. Unfortunately, due to our fallen nature, there is no such thing as "innate good" within a human being, and in the exhaustive search for it the analyst uncovers yet more, or even worse, *badness*. For the elusive innate good, the search is endless, and this is how psychotherapists make their living; by getting their hooks into their patients, many of whom become addicted to the process and revisit time and time again. By the time the ordeal is over, the patient has often become financially bankrupt and possibly a gibbering wreck, all in pursuit of good without God.

---

[3] Interview with the late Dr. William Marra on "Where Catholics Meet" Radio.

THE EVILS OF NAVEL-GAZING

Modern society is permeated with temptations to find one's "inner self" and millions of people are deluded by the idea that, if only they could remove some of the difficulties in their lives, then how happy they would be. The search for this elusive happiness involves the process of shedding those things which we think make us unhappy, such as a bad marriage, a difficult job, or poverty. I once knew a colleague who announced that he was going to participate in a round-the-world yacht race and temporarily abandon his office job in order to "find himself." Alas, after a short time he was struck on the head by a boom and ended up in hospital! The search for earthly happiness is relentless and often involves losing our inhibitions, which results in addictions to popular music, drugs, homosexuality, and many other vices. The result of this phenomenon, which seems to afflict most of society nowadays, is that people are utterly miserable. There are no miserable nuns in Bridget's convent!

WHAT POPE FRANCIS SAYS ABOUT NUNS

In the Clementine Hall of the Papal Palace on January 4, 2025, Pope Francis addresses a gathering of the general chapter of the union of "St Catherine of Siena" school missionaries.

The order comprises Dominican tertiaries, mainly college students or teachers who are, according to their current website, "intending a precise and sympathetic presence of consecrated persons in state schools and in society." The founding members made their first consecration in the cell of St

Dominic at St Sabina's church in Rome in April 1917. The group were aggregated to the order of preachers (Dominicans) and received final papal approval in 1924.

By 1990 the union of St Catherine of Siena had founded many schools and colleges, including the "free university for adults and the elderly," which operates out of many countries including Pakistan, India, Holland, and Poland.

In his speech to delegates of the order, the Holy Father says: "Many times in my life I have encountered nuns with a vinegar face, and this is not friendly, this is not something that helps to attract people. Vinegar is ugly, and nuns with a vinegar face, let's not say!" Pope Francis then continues with the following: "Please, distance yourself from gossip. Gossip kills, gossip poisons. Please, no gossip among you, none. And to ask this of a woman is heroic, but come on, let's go forward, and no gossip."

One can only guess at the information which Pope Francis has received in his pre-meeting briefing by his officials, but at the very least he seems to be under the impression that all is not well with the union of St Catherine of Siena. This is not the first time that nuns generally have been singled out for severe criticism by the Holy Father; convents have had to get used to a constant stream of negative comment from the papal throne. These sentiments have been magnified by certain bishops and have led, in a few cases, to open rebellion by some individual religious houses. The mother superior of the Poor Clares in Belorado, Spain (May 2024) said: "From the Throne of Peter we have been receiving contradiction, confusion and doublespeak, ambiguity, lack of clear doctrine, which is all the more necessary in stormy times, to hold the rudder more firmly." I would venture to suggest, however, that this mother superior, in common with most monastic leaders, is dealing with difficulties which are largely self-inflicted. Many of these religious houses are already weakened by their loss of purpose, leading to internal divisions and lack of vocations.

Pope Francis is aware of the universal crisis of vocations amongst the female orders and, to confirm this, we witness the following exchange during his address on January 4: "And I see that young nuns are lacking! How many novices do you have in the world?" Someone answers: "A dozen."

The warnings to the nuns against gossip and vinegar faces do not really address the basic crisis in the religious orders, both male and female, which is the wholesale lack of recruitment. Who wants to be a monk or nun these days? Why should a youngster give his or her life to Christ when the very spirituality of the monastic life is being undermined and the vows of poverty, chastity, and obedience are habitually sneered at? As congregations are dispersed and monastic property comes under the hammer of the auctioneer, we really do need a reset and must examine the basic principles underlying the religious life.

HOW NUNS USED TO BE

There is a popular notion, given free voice in progressive Catholic circles, which claims that, as religious orders are disappearing, this in itself is proof that we do not need them. But monasticism has always been understood to be essential to the life of the Church. Witness the arrival of the first Carmelite nuns in Notting Hill, London, at the invitation of the then Archbishop of Westminster, Cardinal Manning, in the mid-nineteenth century. The Cardinal established Carmels in each diocese in England and Wales, seeing this as essential to bringing supernatural life into fledgling Catholic communities. He invited these sisters from France long before he considered setting up schools or seminaries. And what did these nuns do when they set up, not knowing a word of English? They prayed, did penance, and begged for food. When they arrived during a rainstorm at their tumbledown house, all they had to eat were a few sandwiches prepared for their journey. Before long at least two of them had died of malnutrition. All these events are described in a book called *In the Silence of Mary: The Life of Mother Mary of Jesus, Carmelite Prioress and Foundress.*[4]

The Catholic Church when the Carmelites arrived in England in 1874 was doing better than it had done at any point since the Reformation, but it was still often a social stigma to be Catholic, and not all doors were open.[5] This was the age of Charles

---

4 London: Carmel of Notting Hill, 1964.
5 In the eighteenth century, Catholics could become solicitors, though not barristers, and there was no impediment to their entering the medical or any other profession. Restrictions were mainly to do with the universities, Parliament, and government service. Catholics were allowed to serve in the armed forces, in the ranks, from 1778, and to hold commissions from 1816. By 1874 the senior Catholic in the British Army was Major-General Henry Clifford, who had won the VC in the Crimea, and the Catholic Russell Manners had been made an admiral in 1855. Catholic Emancipation permitted Catholics to

Dickens and there was a massive divide between rich and poor. The Anglican Church was the bastion of privilege and wealth, while many ordinary people never bothered with any religion at all. A hopeless situation, one would have thought! And yet, from the Carmelites of Notting Hill website we read the following: the Carmel "was intended, in the ardent spirit of St Teresa of Avila, to be a spiritual powerhouse for the evangelisation of England. The little community began in poverty and obscurity, but by the beginning of the twentieth century it was attracting an amazing number of new vocations, women from all walks of life."

The Carmelites who arrived in London in 1874 had no internet, mobile phones, or printing press and were unable to undertake a nationwide program of evangelisation, even if they wanted to. So how did they manage to be so successful? The answer is that God did it all! The nuns' faithfulness to their rule was rewarded a thousand times over. This gives us a hint as to the reasons for the current autodemolition of the monastic orders.

TRADITION WORKS

It is also worth considering the growing number of religious orders, particularly in France, that have returned to their roots. One example is the Benedictine monastery at Le Barroux, in Provence, which is burgeoning with vocations. Any visitor to their Sunday Mass cannot but be over-awed by

---

become barristers in 1829, and by 1861 the first Catholic judge had been appointed. By 1874 the Catholic population of England and Wales was at least 800,000, having grown vigorously from 80,000 in 1780.

the long and endless procession of young monks at the start of the ceremonies. Even the abbot looks like a film star! These monks have no "pastoral outreach" initiatives and make absolutely no compromise with the outside world. The abbey church is packed full of faithful Catholics on Sundays, and the daily Mass is well attended also. The monks also run an oblate program for lay people. Other traditional orders around the world also testify to the swelling of their ranks.

But what's the point, one might ask? Unless these monks and nuns are active in the world and are doing good works, then, surely, they're wasting their time? The evidence points the other way, though: it seems that monks and nuns who set out to "do good" and in doing so neglect the life of poverty, chastity, and obedience, risk turning themselves into pious social workers. Before long they find themselves embracing or compromising with the values of the modern world and any new vocations just fall away. Once monks and nuns become wrapped up in the cares of the world, as Pope Francis says, "vinegar faces and gossip" become an unwelcome ingredient of their conventual life. The intervention of psychotherapy was necessary during the 1960s in order to destroy the monastic orders whose members at that time were bound by their vows, which had to be diluted. Nowadays, however, monks and nuns can save themselves from paying psychotherapy fees because all they have to do is abandon the life of prayer, reimagine themselves as "do-gooders," and go out into the world. The ancient spirituality of monasticism has been long abandoned.

There is an unpleasant truth behind the collapse of the monastic orders within the post-Vatican II Church: having read the testimonies of various ex-nuns who tried their vocations in the 1960s and 1970s, it is obvious that the rot set in when they abandoned the traditional Latin Mass and the traditional Divine Office. I can prove this because there is overwhelming evidence that returning to the traditional Mass and Office has halted the process of decay and put it into reverse. This fact explains why the progressives in the Catholic Church want to destroy the old stuff—they know how potent it is!

CHAPTER 14

Health Issues and Other Turmoils

2019: MAKING FRIENDS WITH MR PARKINSON

I am no longer a financial adviser, thanks to the edicts of the trustee in bankruptcy and also to my Parkinson's disease which has affected my speaking voice. I am now unable to sound coherent over the telephone. Once a financial adviser and his telephone are parted, that is effectively the end. I fill my day by doing what my health allows me in the garden, although my abilities are decreasing owing to lack of balance. I am also writing the draft of *Two Families* and writing articles for Catholic journals. I say five decades of the rosary, three times during the day as there is so much, not only to pray for, but also to be thankful for. I have at least three books on the go which I am reading and always start my day with a chapter from a spiritual tome which has no pictures in it.

I have abandoned the piano stool because of my body's habit of uncontrollable swaying, so much so that I finally fell off and landed on an electric heater. The heater is still in use but has a bottom-shaped dent in it.

When my mother was interviewed by Sir Harry Secombe during his visit to Wells, for an episode of *Highway*, he asked her about her health. Although it was undiagnosed, I am now certain that she was also suffering from Parkinson's disease. She answered that it was as though she was being constantly chased by the illness, and she spent a lot of her time devising ways to keep a few steps ahead as the symptoms advanced. I now know exactly what she means. Parkinson's disease covers a wide range of symptoms; those poor people who have it worse than me find themselves with uncontrollable tremors. Fortunately, neither I nor my mother suffered from those. The "Bevan Parkinson's," experienced by my elder brother David, Ma, and me, is more of a weakness in muscles, especially the legs, causing a lack of balance. Our speaking voices are also weak, and we are given to mumbling.

There is currently a school of thought, particularly amongst medical experts in the United States, which maintains that Parkinson's is largely a disease of the mind and can be overcome, but not cured obviously, by determination. I agree with this to a certain extent, but because it is my automotive actions which suffer the most, I am able to resolve a few difficulties through willpower. For instance, I cannot do more than one thing at a time. If I am walking along, it is impossible to speak to a fellow walker without finding myself unable to carry on walking. If I am having a discussion with a person, I find that I cannot respond quickly to him without my words coming out garbled, so I always have to prepare what I am going to say and speak carefully.

This turns me into a longwinded bore and, as a result, I find it hard to engage at gatherings. Having spent most of my life indulging in hot debate, I now find that I have to shut up. This makes me appear wise, which I am not: *Si tacuisses, philosophus mansisses* (If you had been silent, you would have remained a philosopher). Thus, in life, I think, God sometimes gives us what we deserve! As the French say: "Le bon Dieu est bon!"

PARKINSON'S DISEASE IS SPIRITUAL

Although I have confidence in Almighty God to keep me from acute suffering, I do not demand from him a divinely inspired cure. This is because the disease has changed me into a more deliberate and studious person. I regard this as a definite advance, especially in the spiritual life, because during the early days I was rushing around, leaving little space for prayer and study. I have heard about a certain person who, about the same age as me, was diagnosed with Parkinson's, and promptly committed suicide. This is because that poor soul had nothing to live for. If there is no trust in God and His promises, the diagnosis of a terminal illness, or even Parkinson's (which is usually something you die "with" and not "of") makes the bottom fall out of one's *modus vivendi* and that is why suicide, assisted or otherwise, is often considered. When a professional organist, for example, at the summit of his career, having sacrificed everything for his success (including, perhaps, even his marriage), manifests the symptoms of Parkinson's, that is the end of everything he's worked for. As a result, he may be extremely upset or even resentful. Particularly with this disease, it is essential to be tranquil, as any extreme reaction may speed up the process of the illness. So, I claim in all honesty that Parkinson's is sent by God in His attempt to humble us and increase our devotion to Him. For anyone without faith, it could prove a complete disaster. It is through being in love with Our Lord, something I have mentioned many times in *Two Families*, that we should see everything as part of the divine will and coming as a gift from him, even serious illness. It is this secure knowledge which makes us docile, and even thankful, as we endure without complaint or resentment everything which happens to us.

AND ANOTHER THING...

Archbishop Lefebvre wrote his famous little book entitled *An Open Letter to Confused Catholics* back in the early 1970s. I remember my reaction upon being handed it: "But I'm not confused, what rubbish!" Despite the strange goings-on in my local parish in Shepton Mallet, Somerset, I was in no mood to perform a *volte face* and suddenly make a heroic stand in defence of the pre-Vatican II regime. The saintly Archbishop's widely reported condemnations cut no ice with me at the time, nor with anyone else I knew. To be frank, we all thought he was a bit, you know, extreme. I remember at about that time the Catholic *Universe* publishing a commentary on a list of books which it had for sale, one of which was *An Open Letter to Confused Catholics*, describing it as "an interesting theory about the modernists taking over the Catholic Church."

So, what has changed? From my indifference in the 1970s, through a period of giving up religion completely in my university days, I have now arrived at the position of someone who has embraced wholeheartedly the Son of God and the Church which He founded, the Roman Catholic Church. I hasten to preempt the cynic who assumes that I am some kind of "born again" fanatic along the lines of Billy Graham. Not at all: true love of God cannot be emotional but has to be supernatural—not a "funny inside feeling" but a state of complete trust in our creator, an utter reliance on His providence and, above all, a desire to please Him in everything we think, say, and do.

A true love which is completely unselfish, and which exists to a much lesser extent between married couples, guarantees the success of the union. To be able to give, and not count the cost, is paramount in one's relationship with God and it is this gift of love which makes the world go round. Above all, love of God should not be conditional on the receipt of warm inside feelings and other emotional consolations, much beloved of the charismatics.

Coldness and indifference are the chief enemies of the Catholic Faith nowadays. When I talk about religion to my friends and relations, I see in their eyes a blank and bemused stare. Yes, they go to Church—but not if a conflicting Sunday barbecue is in the offing. Unless Catholics pray and ask God for the gift of supernatural love, their religion is utterly vain and a complete waste of time. It is impossible to save one's soul without this gift because it generates a proper prayer life, not simply treating God like a heavenly Father Christmas but prostrating oneself in humility before the heavenly throne. Those who pray are saved; those who do not pray are damned. There, I've said it! (Actually, it was St Alphonsus.)

Catholics have to be *in love* with Our Lord, everything depends on it. Although this love of God is an act of the will, we cannot hope to acquire it on our own and we need divine grace to form and nurture this love. There is plenty to love in Our Lord, such as His perfection and His wisdom. There is also plenty to love in the Catholic Church, such as incense, Palestrina, vestments, and architecture, but these are only aids to supernatural love. It is obvious to me that visiting the New Rite of Mass in one's local parish, listening to out-of-tune guitars or a corny sermon delivered over a faulty loudspeaker system, and then receiving communion in the hand, does not lead one to develop a love of Our Saviour. In a similar way, addiction to Renaissance art or Bach's *St Matthew Passion* will not supply the supernatural love which is essential in order to be a serious Catholic. These features, which really amount to "props," may well engender an emotional love, but we all know how fickle emotions are. The only way to kickstart a spiritual life is to ask God for the necessary humility—God is everything and we are nothing.

"The Faith is absolutely satisfactory to the mind, enlisting all knowledge and reason in its cause... It is completely compelling to any who give it an 'indifferent and quiet audience.'" So wrote Evelyn Waugh, summing up the central claim of St Edmund Campion in his "brag" which was disseminated round the churches in Oxford in 1580. Human beings need to know from whence they came, where they are, and where they are going. Many resist these burning questions by distracting themselves with daily concerns but, deep down, they ponder these issues. When things are going well, they get even more distracted. In bad times they often fall into despair because they conclude that there is nothing out there beyond the here-and-now. What Campion is saying is that the Catholic Church has all the answers.

Now it is obvious to me that the post-Vatican II Church has given up on its divinely mandated mission to teach all nations. Its clergy, from the Holy Father downwards, do not see things in the same way as the sixteenth-century Jesuits such as Campion. Things have reached such a pretty pass nowadays that, far from being the answer to the problems of the world, the Church has become very much part of the problem.

As we observe the melting down of society—and I do not believe there is a single area of human activity that is not now in severe crisis—we really need to abandon human solutions. Every problem in our lives and in the world has a supernatural cause and can only be solved through supernatural means.

When Archbishop Lefebvre wrote his letter to "confused" Catholics, that is exactly what they were— even if they didn't know it at the time. I think we have now graduated from a state of confusion to one of bewilderment. This bewilderment seems to me to be one step away from giving up religion completely. The problem today is that most Catholics do not know their faith as a result of decades of neglect in the education system. Ignorance of the faith inevitably leads to lapsation. The whole process of falling away from religion is hurried on by worldly clergy and extremely offputting liturgies—all perfectly designed to turn most people away from the supernatural.

The tragedy through which we are living is that most people who have been worn down by years of beatings and betrayals at the hands of the modern Catholic Church are by no means in the mood to embrace Catholic Tradition. Most of those who quit the Church never wish to return, and this is because the supernatural graces have been stamped out and they have become enmired in humanism or materialism. I cannot, therefore, expect this memoir to attract the attention of lapsed Catholics, not as if they would bother to read it in any case. I am addressing the vast majority of Catholics who, although still practising their faith, are almost certainly on the slide: down but not quite out.

So, what right have I to lecture other Catholics? My answer is a simple one; I myself have been pulled through the hawthorn hedge backwards and have suffered at the hands of the revolutionaries in the Catholic Church. I know what defeat and misery feels like. I know what it feels like to thirst for something which one cannot quite put one's finger on. I know what religious coldness and indifference feels like and the lapsation which inevitably follows. I know what serious mortal sin feels like and the reluctance to make amends and make my peace with Almighty God. I know what it is like to bear the guilt of sin, which is unaffected by a confession where the priest says "you're just expressing your inner humanity!" I shudder as I remember the feeling of hopelessness as a lapsed Catholic, thinking that I'm now *so* bad that I can never get back. I am just a simple Catholic, perhaps more simple than Catholic, who has worked out for himself the answers to the deep problems in our world, only to find, like Chesterton, that it has all been thought of and said before, and many times over.

If you wish to recover your Catholic faith, not only is the world against you, as it has always been, but so is today's official Catholic Church. Our Holy Father has just announced not only that God wills *all* religions, but that all religions lead to God. If he is telling the truth, why bother to be a Catholic?

Can the Catholic Church now endorse many religions, some of them contradictory? The notion is preposterous. My advice to anyone trying to revive his faith is to ignore the utterings of Pope Francis and his clergy and stick to what the Catholic Church has always and everywhere taught throughout its history. After all, that is what Catholics did up until our present age of mass media. If you pray for your own conversion, God always listens, regardless of the state of your soul. He will answer. Be careful what you wish for, though, because God can turn your whole life upside down!

DEAD CATHOLICS ARE IN HEAVEN, PURGATORY, OR HELL

Our faith comes from God, who can neither deceive nor be deceived. In addition, the Church is not only the Church Militant, here on earth, but also the Church suffering in purgatory, and the Church Triumphant in heaven. Whatever nonsense is coming out of Rome nowadays does not apply to two-thirds of the Catholic Church which is not here on earth. Heaven is a place where faith is transformed into knowledge and hope into possession. In fact we can be sure that the earthly church, the Church Militant, forms a minute part of the body of Christ in terms of numbers of souls, especially when we consider the massive apostasy which we now face. So, Pope Francis has a comparatively tiny audience compared with the bulk of souls who inhabit purgatory and heaven.

Anyone with the goodwill to seek the truth of the Catholic faith will still find it in all its glory by studying the catechism of St Pius X, the lives of saints, the Councils, and the great encyclicals written before the Second Vatican Council (1962–1965). All this is quite an effort and is not helped by the fact that it is almost impossible to find people in the twenty-first century Church who have sufficient knowledge or belief to enable them to pass it on. Now that the formal teaching apparatus of the Church has collapsed, every convert to the faith has a story to relate containing chance meetings, good examples of others, and various miracles on the way. It can be a very slow and painful process because there is little encouragement from modern Catholic clergy and lay people who have been told by Pope Francis that converting someone is tantamount to sinfulness. Conversion to the true faith often marks the convert out for persecution to varying degrees. When my wife and I embraced the faith and left the modern Church many years ago, we found that we lost the intimacy of our own families and experienced coldness and even aggression. Fortunately,

God sent us a traditional priest to help and guide us. Without his assistance and prayers, I doubt we would have stayed the course.

The Church's abandonment of its teaching authority and its almost institutionalised sense of self-doubt have led to a fragmentation in belief amongst good Catholics. This is because they are largely self-taught and have not received the Faith from a living authoritative source, such as a priest. This has caused divisions even among traditional Catholics, who can be like sheep without a shepherd. Even the very best and knowledgeable ones fail to distinguish between infallible doctrine and their own opinion. They are quick to assert their own opinions without bothering to find out what the teaching of the Church is on a particular matter. It is also very hard for intelligent people to acquire the habit of submission to the higher truths. Conversely, it is often the case that Catholics get on their high horse and speak authoritatively on matters upon which the Church has not definitively pronounced.

THE TEACHINGS OF THE MODERN CHURCH ARE UNREASONABLE

The first and most important fact about our Catholic faith is that it is obviously true. The second fact is that, because the teaching is true, it must be utterly reasonable. A religion which is not reasonable has to find alternative means to hold its faithful to itself, such as superstition, human perversion, or violence of some kind. We are now faced with the reality that the Catholic faith after Vatican II is no longer reasonable, and this is because of a number of concessions made by the Council fathers to the ideals of the world and non-Catholic religions. For example, if the Church of Christ "subsists" in the Catholic Church (an assertion of Vatican II's *Lumen Gentium*), then by implication it can exist in other religions also. Therefore, the Catholic Church is not *necessarily* the one true Church of Christ. If this is so, then we may as well all pack up and go home because, as Our Lord says, "It is no longer good for anything, except to be thrown out and trampled underfoot" (Mt 5:13). The point is that, if the Catholic Church, by its own admission, is not *necessarily* the one true religion, then why on earth would anyone want to convert to it? The grace of conversion relies on a man's natural goodwill and reason leading to openness to the faith. But this natural goodwill and reason would be tested to destruction by the proposition that the Catholic Church is but one religion amongst many, including non-Christian religions. The sort of converts coming into the Church nowadays (and I have met some of them) say "I've become a Catholic because all my friends are Catholic." Or, "My new parish priest says I can just carry on as I was when I was C of E[1] without bothering about any new teachings!" I am sure that we have all heard similar sentiments from friends and relations—and Vatican II is largely to blame. It is small wonder that such converts often do not persevere.

Another fact which stares us in the face is that the Church of Pope Francis represents a complete novelty and a break from the past. Therefore, it is essential

---

[1] Church of England.

that the traditional Mass has to be sidelined and, ultimately, banned. Of course it has! Why do people still blindly think that they're being treated unfairly? The Novus Ordo Mass reflects the the Catholic Church's new religion and all those who question or criticise either one had better get out of the Church. We are actually faced now with the reality of *schism* on the part of the official Church, and this may be God's way of sorting out the mess. The readily identifiable schismatic Church may well sail away and set up on her own and, ultimately, fall apart, for that is what schismatic groups do. Knowing that two-thirds of the Church, in purgatory and heaven, do not go along with Pope Francis is a great comfort and reassurance that all will ultimately be well because all the modernists will have left the Church.

DIVIDED TRADITIONALISTS

One hesitates to predict the breakup of the Church because it flies in the face of Our Lord's promise that the gates of hell will not prevail. However, it is hard to see how the Church can remain united in the face of Pope Francis's onslaught, the effects of which strongly continue. The crux of the problem is that most of the rebels nowadays were perfectly happy with the Vatican II revolution but are now saying that enough is enough and "stop the revolution, I want to get off!" Had they bothered to read the Vatican II documents, which are the *Mein Kampf* of the upheavals, they wouldn't claim that what is now happening is anything new. Of course, very few people took the trouble to read the documents of the Council and were happy to drift along promoting the "spirit" of Vatican II. But going along with all the changes since 1965 yet objecting to what is happening now seems to be illogical, since everything is contained in the documents. All the modern "rebels" in the Catholic hierarchy to a greater or lesser extent accept the revolution in the Church and accept the basic tenets of the Council; that was how they got made bishops and cardinals in the first place! They can hardly begin to denounce the teachings of Vatican II after having profited from loyalty to that Council. To hark back to the "good old days" of Pope John Paul II and Pope Benedict is to completely misunderstand and minimise the depth of the current crisis. The only people acting logically are Pope Francis and the Society of St Pius X, in whose name Archbishop Lefebvre warned us of the forthcoming explosions over fifty years ago. He had studied the Council documents in detail, and I've seen the original *schemata* of the Council preserved in a bookshelf in his bedroom at Ecône—the ones that were ditched by the liberals at the start of the first session.

As news emerges of differences of opinion within certain Catholic dissident organisations and the subsequent ill-tempered exchanges between them, one cannot resist the conclusion that outside the Society of St Pius X, there is widespread confusion and disagreement about the causes of the crisis in the Church.

THEY LOVE ARCHBISHOP LEFEBVRE...BUT AVOID SSPX

The most potent cause of controversy is identifying the root of this crisis, for some say that we haven't had a Pope since Pius XII, others say we haven't had one since Benedict XVI, that Pope John Paul was a conservative saint, that Vatican II and the New Mass are fine so long as we get rid of the abuses and, finally, SSPX is in schism—which was confirmed by Cardinal Burke. But without the Society the Church would have succeeded in destroying its liturgy and beliefs back in the 1970s and '80s. It is a wonderful gift of Divine Providence that we have a generation of priests, religious, and laymen who have fought bravely against the destructive forces of "progress" within the Church. A clear indicator of the confusion is the reluctance of most conservative publishers to disseminate traditionalist articles and books because they are terrified of upsetting the official Church authorities, upon whose goodwill they often depend for their very existence. It very much looks as though conservative Catholic publications will only print contributions which praise Archbishop Lefebvre, whilst avoiding the promotion of SSPX. I regret to add that many articles get rejected by editors on the ground that it "unfortunately does not conform with our current editorial policy." Until the expanding band of "cancelled" priests and bishops starts calling a spade a spade and faces up to realities, the Roman authorities will make quick work of them when the time comes and brush them aside. This is how their loyalty to the Roman authorities is repaid. If you accept even one miniscule revolutionary principle (such as the one promoted by the esteemed art critic, the late Sister Wendy Becket, that Our Lord did not know He was the Messiah until His baptism at the River Jordan), you become part of the problem and not part of the solution. Hence, the oft-proclaimed cry of "unite the clans" is nonsense because these "clans" are scattered by division over important issues. Let us not forget that all the dissident priests and bishops have been trained in the Vatican II Church and have not received the traditional formation which is available in the SSPX seminaries, and thus, their formation is usually defective. I often hear dissident anti-Francis people speak of tradition as a lifestyle choice and not the most essential ingredient for our salvation. Why else do priests happily say both the old Mass and the new Mass without blinking?

SO WHAT'S GOING TO HAPPEN?

The final battle may not be long in coming and may result in the Catholic Church on earth being reduced to a fraction of its size but with truth, beauty, and holiness back where it belongs—in the heart of the Church. We must pray earnestly that the Holy Father, whoever he is at the time, receives sufficient grace to remain in the Church to help with its rebirth after the modernists have set up on their own, and perhaps this is how Our Lord's promise to St Peter will bear fruit.

Having read over the paragraph above I have this uneasy feeling that the crisis in the Church is now so bad that it cannot be resolved by mere human endeavour, such as a Mass on the top of a mountain in Africa, a huge pilgrimage to Chartres, or endless videos on YouTube. I believe deep down that the antidote to the crisis is physical martyrdom, following in the footsteps of our Catholic forefathers and in imitation of our divine master. Anything less will not solve anything. Physical persecution of traditional Catholics is perhaps not as far-fetched as one might imagine, for it would be the simplest thing in the world for the Vatican to ask secular governments to add this small but noisy band to their ever-increasing list of banned groups.

CHAPTER 15

"Something Rotten in the State of Denmark"

2020: WOKERY, THE LATEST TYRANNY

We are entering the ordeal of the COVID pandemic, when we are all encouraged (ordered) to stand outside our houses and applaud the heroic warriors working in the National Health Service (NHS). I refuse to indulge in this ostensibly harmless activity and made to feel very awkward, even unpatriotic, by my more compliant and law-abiding friends. I refuse to cooperate, not because I have any reservations about the NHS—I have none whatsoever—but I always react badly to group pressure. In any case, to stand outside my front door and applaud the passing cars seems to be madness in the extreme. One is reminded of a common situation in Nazi Germany when many people were arrested for failing to toast the Führer on his fiftieth birthday. Might we eventually see the arrest and detention of anyone of whom the state disapproves, such as in Stalinist Russia? With the current atmosphere of mob rule, or "social censorship" as others have termed it, one has to be very careful of one's opinions even in the privacy of one's own home, especially if one is entertaining people who are not very well known. At a dinner party with friends I sometimes feel that some things are better left unsaid, not because I have particularly outrageous opinions, but because one may be misunderstood, and the wrong impression may be given during the ebb and flow of conversation around the dinner table. Thus, we have to leave off controversial subjects such as homosexuality, transgenderism, and anything to do with religion. So, what else is there to talk about? The weather, holidays, and money! One can discuss politics, of course, but only bland statements are acceptable, such as "we need more women in parliament."

With the proliferation of electronic media there has arisen a powerful force within society which is instantaneous and deadly in its effect. This is known as popular opinion or, more accurately, mob rule. Fear of the mob is governing almost every facet of our human existence, and has given rise to an elaborate defence mechanism, which is "political correctness" or "wokery."

WE ARE ALL "WOKE"

Wokery is resorted to in order to neutralise the threat of adverse popular opinion and it affects almost everything we do, say, or think. There is little doubt that there now operates a herd mentality which is driven by the internet. Definitions of "political correctness" or "wokery" have proved elusive simply because it is something we accuse others of, and rarely do we admit that we ourselves are guilty of it. Yet I would suggest that we are as woke as the rest of them and we cannot help being so for the sake of self-preservation. If enough people gang up and assert some opinion or fact, then that opinion or fact often becomes treated as an infallible truth and it would take an extremely courageous person to contradict it, even in private. The mob which clamoured for the death of Our Lord in front of Pontius Pilate has its modern equivalent in the "Twitterstorm" which bays for the "cancellation" of a certain individual who perhaps made an ill-advised remark ten years ago on Facebook. Politicians, even here in the United Kingdom, fear mob rule because it can put them out of business faster than you can say "Twitter." On the other hand, with careful manipulation through the use of marketing men and image-makers, politicians can harness public feeling, as evidenced in electronic media, and achieve positions of unchallenged power.

Long before the arrival of internet-based communications, whipping up mass hysteria had been the speciality of many political leaders in the twentieth and twenty-first centuries. Once the politicians have achieved power, they use the mass media to ensure that they stay in power and are able to do this by adopting a drip-feed campaign of vilification of their political rivals. We often find nowadays that the law, far from guiding our citizens and preventing wrongdoing, is more concerned with following the loudest voices. The expansion of the concept of "Hate Crime" is very worrying because it is utterly ruthless in its operation. The law is not designed to take account of individual circumstances and now we can be punished by the state for our thoughts if we translate them into words. The recent incarceration of a housewife in her sixties, who had never been in trouble with the law, because of some ill-judged and hastily deleted comments on the internet, shows mob rule at its most virulent. I guess that it will not be very long before it will be a criminal offence to support the idea of slavery, for example, which is understandable: who but a lunatic would actually support slavery? But the next law to come in might make it a criminal offence not to criticise slavery when called upon to do so.

EXTRA-JUDICIAL MOB RULE

So wokery has led to the founding of a huge mass of unwritten rules, the breaking of which leads to consequences which can be far more extreme and far beyond the powers of our courts. This unwritten law uses certain powerful adjectives which, when applied to a particular individual, can have a devastating effect. Such words include "racist," "homophobic," "misogynist," "xenophobe," and "far right." The list is endless, and new words emerge every day but, above all, there is the "catch-all" condemnatory epithet *"inappropriate."* We hear about a university lecturer, for example, who had been suspended for making "inappropriate" remarks during a tutorial. The vagueness is chilling and deadly because it reminds us of the dictum, "give a dog a bad name." He would be unable to defend himself because the accusation is so vague yet, at the same time, deadly enough to ruin his career.

In 2023, an English sports commentator and former national team captain was suspended by the BBC from his commentary job because of alleged "inappropriate" remarks overheard in the team dressing room in 2009. He was one of the lucky ones as the complaint was not upheld, but one can only imagine how he felt as he contemplated his long and distinguished career in ruins. One might ask why and how an overheard unguarded comment in a remote cricket changing room resulted in such a public outcry. It all started from a leaked report by a casual eavesdropper who, no doubt, was keen to assert his own political credentials. As an avid cricket fan and listener to cricket commentary on the radio, I often wonder what the fate of a commentator would be who used the word "batsman" rather than the preferred new word, "batter" (why do I always think of cod and chips?); we would probably never hear from him again.

In another example, a well-known historian who was a media personality and a personal acquaintance of mine made an ill-judged remark during an interview and was summarily "cancelled." It was the resulting Twitter *tempête* that lost him his publishing contract; he was also deprived of his fellowship of a Cambridge college and was no longer welcome as a guest on public service television and radio. Such extra-judicial penalties are worthy of the Nazis, yet it was all the result of mob rule leading to such unconfined and universal rage that it almost seemed as though only a public hanging would have satisfied it. One can be confident that none of these people would ever, ever repeat such remarks knowing, as they now do, the probable consequences.

One of the features of cancellation is that apologies are more or less useless and often counterproductive. Mob rule, by its very nature, is a national sport and nothing is allowed to come between the mob and its prey. People who participate in this sport, and there are millions of them, are often motivated by *schadenfreude*, which is the pleasure derived from observing the discomfiture and downfall of others. Cancellation is also a national sport in which the participants are, on the one side, public or semipublic figures and, on the other side, a baying bloodthirsty mob of idle mobile phone addicts. This has many similarities with the Roman amphitheatres which staged public one-sided pitched battles for the entertainment of the population. In times of economic hardship these events were a useful diversion which, at least for a short time, stopped the citizens from thinking too hard about their own deprivations. In George Orwell's famous novel 1984, where the party whipped up hatred against an imaginary enemy, the intended effect was to unite the population behind the oppressive government.

WE'RE NEXT

The running down and persecution of sportsmen, politicians, and historians is bad enough, yet history tells us that there are people who tick all the boxes in terms of public vilification: the Roman Catholics. Just to be clear, I am talking about the modern post-Vatican II Church here. The corruption of the Church after the council and the attempt to modernise it will cut no ice with its future persecutors and this is because the persecutors are doing what they do out of blind prejudice. When the time comes, to admit that one is a Catholic could be sufficient to attract deprivations, which may include imprisonment and death, just as it has throughout the whole of history. It will be no use claiming that, although one is Catholic, one believes in freedom of conscience, religious liberty, and ecumenism, as this will probably infuriate one's persecutors to greater outrages. The only escape will be as it has always been: to deny Christ openly and without the possibility of contradiction. The tragedy is that few Catholics will be prepared to suffer persecution, a great grace and a gift from God, having been softened up over the last sixty years on a diet of the new Mass and its accompanying errors.

We are well on the way to open persecution of the Catholic Church in the West. This persecution is getting closer because already we hear strident anti-Catholic views from all corners of society, loudly proclaimed by the likes of Professor Richard Dawkins, Sir Steven Fry, and Mr Matthew Parris, all of whom are brilliant anti-Catholic orators whose tub-thumping "no-popery" orations are in popular demand in televised public debates. For those who are less quick off the mark intellectually, there are also the outpourings of Mr Ricky Gervais, who says that he believes in science rather than religion. All these speakers can be found on YouTube, if one can be bothered to have a look, but it is worth mentioning that Mr Fry's debate on the Catholic Church nine years ago has attracted over six million views. Anti-Catholicism has been described as the last permitted prejudice and one clever way the Church gets persecuted is by the media putting up its favourite anti-Catholic rabble-rouser to have a debate against some thick and ill-informed Catholic who is unable to defend his position. I know a number of priests and laymen who could easily send Messrs Dawkins, Fry, Parris, and Gervais packing, but nothing of the kind is ever allowed to happen, and that is persecution.

The reason that Catholicism comes in for so much prejudice has not changed since the Church's foundation: it is the fact that the Church is, by definition, in a state of enmity with the world. In fact, true Catholics say that if they are approved of by the world then they are not being proper Catholics. As Sebastian Flyte maintains in *Brideshead Revisited*, what is important to Catholics is not important to the world and what is important to the world is not important to Catholics. It is this feature of Catholicism which creates an impression of being alien to outsiders, almost as though Catholics do not really belong in the world—which they do not!

OUR BISHOPS ARE RUNNING SCARED

It is the fear of persecution, electronic or otherwise, which is probably behind the words and actions of Pope Francis and the Catholic clergy in general. The Holy Father must know that he has to keep on the right side of the media and how quickly it can destroy him. If this is the case, then how on earth can he possibly preach true faith and morals? He and his fellow bishops are now in an impossible position as having to sideline or even deny authentic Catholic teaching simply out of self-preservation. The tragedy is that this attempt to popularise Catholic teaching can only end in tears, as we know how fickle the world is. We are now living in the world of Wokery, where true opinions are smothered in favour of bland neutrality. One has only to listen to any political debate on the airwaves to notice how dumbed-down the standards have become. In fact, it is so bad that one can almost predict everything which is said and the temptation to switch off the radio is overpowering. There is no doubt that most people are terrified into silence or meaningless clichés to such an extent that debate about the real problems facing the world is stifled. The synod on synodality and the resulting "flannel" at its press conferences is entirely the result of terror of the mob.

Will Pope Francis or his successor reach a point where he says "enough is enough" and start the fightback? I doubt it. In any case, let us hope that God will intervene before there is a final confrontation. We, as Catholics, have our part to play if God is going to put things right, and that is to perform our simple duties of state and be in a state of grace. Humanly speaking, the situation is hopeless as we cannot turn the clock back and return to some kind of sanity on our own. History has shown us that when civilisations become corrupt, they never halt in their course of self-destruction. That is because the crisis in the Church and the world, from which we are now suffering, has a supernatural cause and therefore requires supernatural remedies.

CHAPTER 16

Confusion Reigns

2025: A SUGGESTED ANSWER TO OUR ILLS: WITHOUT GOD

I am listening to the latest Richard Dimbleby lecture at the BBC which, this year, is given by Sir Gareth Southgate. This gentleman was one of the most successful managers of the English football team and his wide experience of football spans at least thirty years. He delivers his speech in a languid and self-effacing manner which is very appealing. Although the title of his talk, delivered to a cross section of the great and the good at London University, is absent, he very eloquently describes his dealings with youngsters both in and outside his chosen game. Southgate astonishes me with his detailed analysis of the hopelessness of the young, buried as they are, he says, in electronic media and often lacking in ambition and drive. I am shocked by his claim, backed up by the Centre for Social Justice, that suicide is now the chief cause of death amongst those aged below fifty. So, more people kill themselves than are victims of road accidents, or even smoking. Just as worrying is his assertion that over fifty percent of children grow up in single-parent households.

Although he is depressingly accurate in his analysis of the breakdown of our society, particularly with reference to youngsters, he is rather muddled and vague in his suggestions for a remedy. The remedies which he proposes disappear in a cloud of aphorisms and clichés. Much is made of "self-determination, self-respect, ambition, drive, and role models." All this is very well, coming from a very rich self-made man with a wife and family. Alas, for a kid from a broken family living on a council estate, who spends most of his time indulging in online gaming and other more depraved internet activities, Sir Gareth really has no answer at all.

In order to make spiritual advances, and thus cure all the evils in society, I believe that we have to identify the common enemy and arm ourselves against it, otherwise we will fail in any attempt to make progress, as a deadly enemy lurks behind every tree. This enemy is *Life without God* (LWG). LWG presupposes that we can live out our lives happily and fruitfully without God or, one may say, assume that we can have "good without God" (GWG).

So where do we find good if not in God? The philosophers down the centuries have struggled with this question and have tied themselves up in knots over it. However, during the eighteenth century and the "age of Enlightenment," Edmund Burke suggested that goodness is embodied in the law of the land. In those days, perhaps it was. But we are currently living in an age where there are many laws which depart from natural goodness, such as those concerning "gay marriage."

THE LAW IS ALL THAT'S LEFT

Nowadays the law has become a religion in itself and it permeates every aspect of our lives. In the field of financial services, which was my speciality, it is now almost impossible to function as a financial adviser without being suffocated by volumes of regulations governing every corner of the client-adviser relationship. Now, I am not saying that these strictures are unnecessary, although many of them are utterly crass, such as the latest rule that an investment adviser must charge the client at exactly the same hourly rate whether he invests £400 or £4,000,000. This has put many advisers out of business because, if they charge £100 per hour for their work, this will adversely affect the poor client with only £400 to invest, whereas the rich client will not even notice the charge. This means that clients who aren't rolling in money are denied independent financial advice because they cannot afford to pay for it. The lawmakers in this case have decided that it is a bad principle for advisers to charge a percentage of the amount invested. Their rationale is that advisers cannot be expected to deal honestly with clients and use their common sense. This is probably justified given the common assumption that advisers usually operate by the LWG principle and are therefore untrustworthy. Overregulation is designed to prevent the "baddies" from cheating the public, which could be fine, but all this does is to drive the good and honest people out of the industry whilst leaving the crooks to get round the regulations as usual. That's the trouble with the law, it cannot take human circumstances into account and is, by its very nature, blind. One of the problems with the "religion" of law, which is worshipped in the law courts, is that it involves a cat-and-mouse game where the rich, ably assisted by overpaid lawyers, try to get round the law.

So far as the criminal law is concerned, it is not the fear of punishment which stops people from committing crimes; rather, it is the likelihood of getting caught. In my case, and no doubt for the readers of this book, we would never contemplate committing even the smallest crime on principle. But for the many hundreds of thousands of petty criminals, the only deterrent is the prospect of detection. This is all thanks to LWG. The reluctance to offend the law should be as a result of love of God, and the resulting love of one's country and its institutions, not the fear of detection and certainly not the fear of punishment. There is scant evidence that the fear of punishment is in any way a factor in deterring criminal behaviour. Perhaps the death penalty prevented a few murders but, of course, murder is not such a widespread problem, and most murders are committed in the heat of the moment. The worst affliction upon society is petty theft and no one is suggesting hanging those offenders. (An anecdote: I am told that there was a rash of housebreaking in Germany in the 1930s and Hitler introduced the death penalty for such miscreants. It certainly solved the problem).

LET'S ALL BE NICE

LWG has had one overriding effect on modern society: more and more laws are being passed to force us to be nice to each other. In more sober times, to make a racist remark was regarded as being in bad taste and most people adopted a form of self-censorship. More importantly, though, racism is a sin which would have to be confessed. Some years ago, I was travelling in a taxi which I shared with two work colleagues in central London. I was listening to the two men chatting and was quite appalled by the racist remarks they made. To make such remarks nowadays, even in private, would be unthinkable and that is because of the force of new laws. What one forgets is that those two colleagues probably still hold the same opinions but refrain from expressing them for fear of legal penalties and public disgrace. One cannot expect the force of law to make people good and change their minds. The best the law can achieve is to bottle up prejudice and drive debate underground and I dread the day when people are unable to restrain themselves any longer and openly rebel against "hate laws." Unless people obey the law because they *want* to rather than because they *have* to, such laws may well turn out to be unenforceable. If a certain law is only obeyed because of the fear of detection or punishment, and not because of love of one's country, such a law may well end up being honoured more in its breach. With the repressive "hate laws" now coming into force, which curb the desire to speak openly and frankly about a variety of issues, we often hear about inadvertent "slips of the tongue," which result not only in prosecution but also in social disgrace and, ultimately, cancellation.

Despite the obvious shortcomings of our laws and our legal system, as outlined above, one cannot help but notice how the vast majority of the populations of civilised countries worship the law. During the early sixteenth century, the mediaeval love and worship of God was replaced by the new religion of "progress." Hand in hand with this development came the massive invasion of new laws and in England it was the Tudors who used such laws to maintain themselves in power and enforce their religious settlement. The murderous "show trials" during the reign of Henry VIII, and the kidnappings and torture by the secret police under Sir Francis Walsingham during the reign of Elizabeth I, were all worthy of the Gestapo. These happenings were received with indifference by most of the English populace, who were happy to go along with the new oppressive regime. It is hard, even nowadays, to imagine what it must have been like to be forced to attend the new Protestant services on pain of fines, deprivation, or imprisonment. Yet apart from one layman, St Thomas More, and one bishop, St John Fisher, the Protestant settlement was broadly accepted. The two rebellions, the Pilgrimage of Grace and the Prayer Book Rebellion, were crushed by mercenaries brought in from Europe. The laws introduced by the Tudors were utterly different from those commonly accepted by the population during the Middle Ages. For in mediaeval England the only laws which meant anything were the laws of treason, and in most cases, this was something which affected the nobility. A peasant would have no idea about treason but would have a working knowledge of the natural law as contained in the ten commandments.

As he was more fearful for the state of his soul, the average peasant in, say, the thirteenth century would not normally indulge in what we now call "petty crime." All this changed, however, with the arrival of the Tudor monarchs whose laws, for the first time in history, compelled certain courses of action on the part of their subjects, such as being forced to go to the reformed church services. These oppressive laws soon had the effect of blunting the average citizen's love and goodwill towards the state. With the advent of real poverty, caused by the dissolution of the monasteries, there grew up a burgeoning class of outcasts who were lawless and unemployed. That is what the growth and expansion of the law did: it created an underclass of people who were indifferent to the norms and values of those who had a stake in society. This is explained in detail in *The English Reformation* by William Cobbett. Bereft of any religious education, these people ended up either in the Victorian workhouses or they starved to death, whilst at the top of society gentlemen thrived in huge estates with limitless wealth which had been stolen from the Catholic Church during the Tudor era. The opulent lifestyles adopted by even the Anglican clergy, as described in the novels of Anthony Trollope, produced a bogus class system based on wealth and land which we are still living through today. Even a cursory reading of many nineteenth-century novels, such as those of Jane Austen, will give us a clear picture of the idle rich who lived off the fat of the land, misused their tenants, and often never did a stroke of work in their lives.

Now it isn't my intention to preach class war and condemn people for living in idleness or in extreme poverty, evil as these things are. My point is that the moral stuffing was knocked out of society at the time of the Reformation and people turned from what was important—the desire to be united with God in communion with the Catholic Church—to secondary matters, such as the advance of human progress. It was this human progress which has failed to live up to expectations by producing a divided society under oppressive governments. All these problems in society are a direct result of LWG, producing as it has a sickness which is incurable. We cannot turn back the clock in any general sense and governments are powerless to act—not that they would want to anyway, because they can only pass laws, and we already know how counterproductive social legislation has become.

THE TRAGEDY OF THE YOUNG

I have introduced Mr Google-Brain previously and I would describe this gentleman as someone who has replaced rational, critical, and independent thought with slogans and aphorisms, and this is the result of addiction to electronic media. He is in a state of intellectual paralysis. There has now grown up a huge and emergent underclass of human beings who are regarded as amoral consumers and, far from rebelling against the moral law, never knew it in the first place. These are grandchildren of those who rebelled against authority in the 1960s and 1970s and the children of those who compromised or rejected religion completely. They may not even have a dad and a mum living with them because they are born out of wedlock and many are not baptised, still less are they likely to be taken to church. It is this phenomenon which Sir Gareth Southgate laments so much. This burgeoning generation of children I can only describe as aliens, and we must be prepared to pay a heavy and bitter price for our negligence over the last fifty or so years. Rules of conduct which have been inherited from our ancestors, and either watered down or rejected by our parents and grandparents, will cut no ice with the new alien class. These inheritors of our neglect and foolishness will have their own version of GWG and very unpleasant it may be for those who are still attached to the past.

Having read and enjoyed *A Perfect Spy*, written by John Le Carre, I am reminded of the communist spymaster, Axel, pouring out his heart to the hero, Magnus Pym. "In the pursuit of peace, we are making too much war. In the pursuit of freedom, we are building too many prisons. But in the long run I don't mind. Because I know this. All the junk that made you what you are, the privileges, the snobbery, the hypocrisy, the churches, the schools, the class system, the historical lies, the little lords of the countryside, the little lords of big business, and all the greedy wars that result from them, we are sweeping that away for ever. Because we are making a society that will never produce such sad little fellows as (Sir) Magnus." A more clear and concise definition of GWG I have not seen, and it matches up perfectly with the developing notion amongst most people that man is born good but ends up being corrupted and made bad by his surroundings. Psychotherapy, a booming industry nowadays, is largely based on this assumption: everything unpleasant in our lives is someone else's fault. To cut a long story short, this is a direct denial of the doctrine of original sin, the bulwark of the Catholic religion.

IT'S THE PRIEST'S FAULT

A traditional priest once told me that behind every social evil in the world lies a bad Catholic priest. One may have to trace back a generation or so but, sure enough, a Catholic priest is lurking. This bald statement requires further explanation. All good comes from God and nowhere else. A Catholic priest represents God on this earth and Our Lord founded the Catholic priesthood to continue His presence here. To put it another way, a Catholic priest is strictly responsible for the salvation of all the souls in his parish, not just the Catholic ones. Likewise, the bishop is responsible for the salvation of all the souls in his diocese. In this way, all good is embodied primarily in the source of all good, which is God, as represented by His priests, many of whom have now given up on the doctrine of original sin. When grandma went to confession to her local priest in, say, 1965, the priest may well have told her, "You can't help it because you're just expressing yourself." After that experience, grandma was hardly likely to imbue her children with the notion of sin. That is why all evil is ultimately laid at the door of faithless Catholic priests.

All human beings are born with the stain of Adam's sin on their souls, and this is removed by baptism. It was not God's original intention to hobble the human race in this way because, when Adam and Eve walked in the garden of Eden, there was no sin. Even the animals loved each other! It was all spoiled because Adam used the precious gift of free will to rebel against God and it was this "first disobedience" which plunged the human race into a state of enmity with God. In order to remedy this sad state of affairs, the Son of God paid the debt of our sin by suffering horribly and founding the Catholic Church. Although we know that baptism removes its stain, original sin leaves us in a weakened state, and we all have a propensity to offend God. So, if we sin nowadays, we are not doomed to hell, which is all we deserve; no, we can visit a darkened church one evening and enter the confessional box. Following an exchange of whispers, one can leave the box having received God's forgiveness for all one's sins. We do not need to lie on the psychotherapist's couch and pay £60 per hour in the forlorn hope of alleviating our guilt, because the services of a priest are free!

ORIGINAL SIN

The greatest evils in the world result from the denial of original sin because people refuse, like the good psychologists they are, to take responsibility for their own shortcomings. A corollary of this attitude is the universal opinion that the individual is right in everything he thinks, says, and does by the very fact that he "feels" that it is right. A form of "self-worship" is the result, evidenced by the simple fact that when a man such as this is challenged, his immediate response is along the lines of "you're disrespecting me and my opinions." In this case it is quite normal for him to claim that any misery he suffers is the result of his upbringing or his poverty and therefore he cannot be held responsible for any of it. Most people deny the existence of original sin by saying that we are born good and free, only to be corrupted by the world. I know for a fact that this is the position of Methodists. In the case of Methodists, as with most Protestant sects, they deny the efficacy of good works because, frankly, the world is so evil that it is all a complete waste of time. All you have to do, as a Methodist, is to proclaim Jesus as your saviour—and bingo! You're saved. This pessimism relating to the world is so intrinsic to Protestantism that they have invented all sorts of devices to circumvent the evils in our lives either by ignoring the world and going to live in a commune, or by living in the world and embracing the evils with open arms, as recommended by Martin Luther.

Poor Sir Gareth Southgate! So clear in his perception of the ills of our society and yet unable to suggest a worthwhile remedy. This is because, dare I repeat myself, such evils are of a supernatural origin and require supernatural remedies. The denial of the supernatural is at the root of the current destruction of society.

DEATH OF A FRIEND

In 2012 there took place an internal split within the SSPX during which Bishop Williamson left the group in protest and set up his own breakaway group, which has, predictably and unfortunately now, in 2025, subdivided into warring factions.

In February of this year, we receive the news that Bishop Williamson has died. In the early days I counted myself one of his friends, as he was a frequent visitor to our house in Dover, and we even played piano duets together. He used to address me as "my favourite chump!" I was happy to endure this well-intentioned insult because, intellectually speaking, he was formidable and miles ahead of me.

There is no doubt about His Lordship's gifts: his culture, his supreme intellect, and his Catholic faith, from which he never wavered even for a moment. Like a "veritable Renaissance Man," he excelled in just about everything he turned his hand to. Early recordings of his conferences must have brought many converts into the Church, as he had the gift of putting across the truths of our religion with beauty and clarity.

Events in the past twenty years have shown a different side to Bishop Williamson. Putting undue emphasis on politics, he started to surround himself with a coterie of followers many of whom were single men harbouring "right-wing" prejudices. It is possible that living in this kind of echo-chamber enabled the Bishop to harden his views. The current crisis in the Church and society as a whole was analysed by means of conspiracy theories and slogans, for Bishop Williamson was very attached to neat oversimplifications. These have enormous appeal to those who are attracted to the comfortable feeling of certainty, and any attempt to counter this "sloganisation" gets dismissed as liberalism.

Bishop Williamson's "Resistance" (as he termed it) eventually acquired a wide membership, mainly thanks to his extensive use of electronic media. By 2013, while rector of the SSPX seminary in the USA, he became convinced that SSPX, and its then superior general Bishop Bernard Fellay, were just about to sell out to Rome under Benedict XVI. This never happened, of course, and yet the bishop was always on the lookout for telltale signs of the predicted betrayal. Every action of the SSPX, including every utterance of its leadership, was interpreted in such a way as to fan the dying embers of this expectation, but to no avail. He will be remembered by his followers, not for his undoubted adherence to the Catholic Faith—which was heroic—but more for his political positioning. Very few obituaries I have seen make even a passing reference to these views, concentrating as they do on his theological teaching, which was obviously impeccable. Yet, to gloss over his historical and political analyses is to present an incomplete summary of his life and works, as only that explains why he was living in a house in Broadstairs rather than in a seminary or bishop's palace.

I have absolutely no doubt whatever, in so far as I am qualified to judge of course, that His Lordship had the Catholic Faith. Yet he was given to rash judgments and, on a few public occasions, made very hurtful remarks about the SSPX in general and Bishop Fellay in particular. When I mentioned to Bishop Fellay, a few years ago, that Bishop Williamson was our new neighbour in Kent, the bishop looked very upset, replying: "He hates me...he really does!" A cursory glance through the internet at some of Bishop Williamson's more notorious lectures and sermons will confirm that his personal opinion of his ex-Superior-General verged on contempt. Allowing his feelings to be aired in such a public and damaging way is not normal in a prince of the Church, whom one expects to be diplomatic and to exercise restraint.

The Bishop's exit from the Society of St Pius X was, I have no doubt, badly handled and peremptory. The SSPX authorities are not trained in any kind of management school and Archbishop Lefebvre was concerned about this from the very start. When someone complained to him about being mistreated by a priest, the Archbishop would shrug his shoulders in that French way and reply, "What can I do? These are heavy responsibilities on young shoulders." I could fill a book with anecdotes about people who were (and are) badly treated by the SSPX. But the anger of Bishop Williamson was so deep and unconfined that he could never bring himself to say anything remotely complimentary about the Society. I do accept, however, that he had retained friendships with various SSPX priests who valued his counsels right up until his last days. However, I have come to regard some of his public statements as pretty outrageous and severely lacking in charity. He had a habit of mockery when describing those who met with his disapproval, mimicking them using a high lispy voice. This is not edifying and takes me to my next point: his opinions about those he termed the "Red Sea crossers." Along with the Holocaust and many other hot issues, these are not topics to be aired in the pulpit—they should be kept private and hidden. However, this was not in his character, thinking, no doubt, that he could shock people out of their liberal ideas. For him and for many of his followers, politics and religion were parts of a seamless garment. Translated, this means that, unless you believe that the Twin Towers in New York were blown up by the CIA, he once maintained, then you're not a proper Catholic!

Long ago, Father Jean-Pierre de Caussade SJ in his book *Self-Abandonment to Divine Providence* repeatedly warned against having a single spiritual director or even relying on a single priest to oversee one's spiritual life. The risks are obvious; suppose that priest says or does something to which you object? This is what happened with Bishop Williamson when a group of his followers fractured and subdivided, some even claiming that *he* was a liberal. And what if the priest (or bishop as in this case) dies? His replacement, if there is one, may not be able to hold things together, as he cannot hope to have the irresistible magnetism of his predecessor.

One of the original priests, who joined the "Resistance" in the early days, eventually left the group declaring Bishop Williamson a "liberal," and managed to get himself consecrated as a bishop. In turn, this new bishop found his own Resistance group split by an internal war and his opponents have set up the Resistance mark III. There is a little band of them in the UK, visited by a priest from the United States, who can only receive the sacraments about once every six weeks. However, they feel comfortable in that they are not tainted by liberal ideas like Resistance marks I and II—not to mention the SSPX arch-liberals. It will probably be only a matter of time before we see more subdividing and it is all because of personal and political allegiances dominating their spiritual lives, rather than adherence to the timeless teachings of the Catholic Church. Would it be too cynical to suggest that they might enjoy the feeling of superiority that belonging to a small, select, and purist band gives them?

An implacable hatred of the SSPX has been inherited by most of the Bishop's surviving followers and they have been so indoctrinated by his worldview that they would often prefer to miss Mass for weeks on end rather than darken the doors of an SSPX chapel.

Every member of the Catholic Church has to possess what is termed a "thirst for souls." The question which I ask is whether these Resistance groups have such a thing, or whether they are merely insular, a select band of brothers? It is doubtful that these groups are expanding because of the anger and bitterness which pervades most of their members. In the case of Bishop Williamson, his public and outspoken rants have had the effect of allowing potential converts to dismiss the whole traditional Catholic movement as a band of nutcases: "a plague on all their houses." If this is Bishop Williamson's true legacy, then it is a tragedy.

CHAPTER 17

The Elusive Peace

THE WHIGGERY-WOKERY VERSION OF HISTORY

The world is holding its breath as we witness the bargaining between the superpowers over Ukraine and Israel and I very much hope that this book does not end up as ashes in a nuclear wasteland!

There is little doubt that the rewriting of history is the favourite pastime of our modern influencers. This is how they impose the concept of "progress" on the historical narrative and, by doing so, change history. This approach was first adopted by the "Whig" historians of the nineteenth century, such as Thomas Macaulay. Anything in history which is contrary to modern concepts of political correctness is either sidelined, denied, or ridiculed, resulting in the sanitisation of certain past events, leading now to even the wholesale destruction of public statues and other reminders of the past. For example. I remember at school how the teacher explained the trial and execution of Charles the First in a manner which I can only describe as tongue-in-cheek. They were all so backward in those days, he maintained, and Charles was represented to us as a rather vain dandy, a naughty boy, who was simply behind the times. Equally, the slave trade in history has been subject to revisionist interpretation and we are confronted with a tyranny of soul-searching from which nothing is safe, not even the effigy of William Colston, the slave owner in Bristol. Richard III is more or less laughed at as a mediaeval Al Capone and Mary Tudor is characterised as a mass murderer. Even the Spanish Inquisition has been raised to the level of the Nazi holocaust. The recent claim that the chief advisers to Edward II, Piers Gaveston and Hugh Dispenser, were "gay" has been accepted without question by many commentators. The notion that two men can love each other deeply in a spiritual sense is lost on modern historians. Thus, the trivialising of history ensures that it is all bunk because it is in the past and, after all, had historical figures known what we know today, then they would not have acted in the way that they did. So, we have nothing to learn from the past, which is presumably why we are condemned to repeat it. And so it is that, nowadays, we have adopted the self-assurance of crusaders, not only by writing off the past but also by attempting to impose on the rest of the world our godless values, such as "democracy" and "freedom of speech."

THE POLICEMEN OF THE WORLD

The United Nations declaration of human rights (1948) states in article 1: "All human beings are born free and equal in dignity and rights. They are endowed with reason and conscience and should act towards one another in a spirit of brotherhood." On the face of it, this clause sounds so reasonable and even moving, yet a more bloodthirsty statement of godlessness one cannot imagine, and this is because it promotes and espouses "good without God." This is, after all, merely an expression of someone's opinion and it has had its predecessors not only in the French Revolution, but also in the United States Declaration of Independence, which says more or less the same thing. In modern times it provides for utterly unjustifiable interventions in Iraq and Afghanistan. Article 1 of the UN declaration provides a green light to the bully boys of western governments to interfere in the affairs of other countries—and to what end? The answer is devastation, starvation, and years of terrorist-driven political unrest. I have heard it said by a political commentator that US foreign policy is based on the assumption that inside every foreigner is an American bursting to get out. This paternalist "we know what's best for Johnny Foreigner" attitude may well be the cause of the final nuclear conflagration, because the superpowers are fighting so many proxy wars all over the world that direct confrontation is inevitable at some stage in the future. The mediaeval English kings had more justification for invading France than Tony Blair's sojourn to Iraq. During the Hundred Years' War, King Edward III (1312–1370) had a justifiable claim to large tracts of French territory, and when he fought the Battle of Crecy (1346) with his son, the Black Prince, it was not in order to install freedom of speech and democracy in France.

THE DESIRE FOR WAR

Now, at the time of writing, the eyes of the world are diverted to the Ukraine where NATO is conducting a proxy war against Russia. How can this possibly end without worldwide conflagration? It is difficult to see. The problem here is that if everyone wants war against Russia, then war is what they will undoubtedly get. One may well remember the timeworn phrase, "be careful what you wish for." Real wars result in the threefold nightmares of Dresden, Auschwitz, and Stalingrad. Are we really prepared for all that, over Ukraine? Sooner or later both sides will have to curb their missionary zeal and gather around the conference table to hammer out some kind of peace deal. Total war nowadays is unthinkable. Now that the horrors of World War Two are no longer within living memory, too many people are willing to "Cry 'Havoc!,' and let slip the dogs of war."[1]

The question which most people are asking is whether Vladimir Putin is the reincarnation of Adolf Hitler and is planning to swallow up one country after another. The point being that, with a nuclear war, we shall never know! I think a face-saving peace settlement, however unjust on both sides, is preferable to annihilation. In fact, it is hard to look at any peace deal in modern times which hasn't involved the humiliation of one side or the other, coupled with huge lingering injustices. I cannot help but remember the price of peace in Northern Ireland, which included the spectacle of republican terrorists being let out of prison in 1997. Those men who murdered Jean McConville, in cold blood, simply got away with it. The resolution of international strife is really nothing of the sort. All it amounts

---

[1] Shakespeare, *Julius Caesar*, Act 3, scene 1, line 273.

to is the cobbling together of face-saving formulae which keep the warring factions apart for a limited period of time. The major obstacle to peace in the Ukraine is mutual hatred; Putin is regarded by Ukrainians as the heir to Stalin who murdered ten million of their fellow countrymen, and the Russians still cannot forget that Ukrainians supported Hitler and supplied the SS with manpower. There is an additional factor, which is the Western powers supplying weapons and fighting their own proxy war against Russia. This is the most perilous aspect of the whole issue and may well lead to the war expanding out of control. Like Iraq and Afghanistan, there is a certain vagueness as to war aims and this is why danger lurks.

We now face intractable and insoluble strife all over the world on the same lines as Ukraine, caused by the underlying desire of mankind to impose his own version of "good" on other countries. This is "good without God." It is godlessness which has led to most of the nations of the world, including every African country, being unable to live with themselves and/or their neighbours. There are now far more wars in the world compared with, say, 1935, and most foreign affairs experts agree that the world nowadays has never been so insecure. World War Three could, in theory, start just about anywhere and could be caused either by NATO enlargement or by Islamic insurgency or, perhaps, both of these things. With many countries now possessing nuclear warheads, the risk of starting an accidental war is dangerously high, given the electronic early warning and automatic retaliation systems now in place.

GOD'S PEACE IS TRANQUILLITY

Without God, peace can be defined only as an absence of war. For there to be genuine peace, there must be complete tranquillity. That cannot happen because it is almost impossible to remove the original causes of the conflict where there is a clash of ideologies rather than a struggle over territory. Politicians who think that they are the architects of "lasting peace" in, say, Northern Ireland, have in fact left a poisonous atmosphere of festering resentment. A casual glance around the world's trouble spots will confirm that real peace, based on tranquillity, is nonexistent, and the mutual burning hatred remains. In spite of countless United Nations peace initiatives and the arrival of peacekeepers with their light blue helmets and rubber guns, all that has happened is a temporary ceasefire, which only erupts into renewed conflict once the newspapers have taken their eyes off the situation. Africa, despite the best efforts of countless peacekeepers, is now mostly a seething cauldron of war, rebellion, and discontent, not to mention famine, poverty, and disease. The continuous strife in African countries has been caused, firstly, by independence struggles against colonial rule, then communism which tore many countries apart in civil war, and, finally, Islamic insurgencies, which are present in most African countries today. Most of these countries are extremely rich in terms of raw materials but the iron ore, diamonds, and coal remain in the earth unharvested whilst the populations starve, and their governments raid the treasury and salt away the wealth into Swiss bank accounts. The many attempts by the United Nations to impose democracy on African countries have resulted in utter failure. This is because power politics in these countries is superimposed on ancient tribal rivalries and these tribes will engage in terror and corruption in order to obtain power and then to hold onto that power for as long as possible. Such people, to whom democracy is an amusing joke, adopt a winner-takes-all approach, so when they win power by whatever means, their promises to mend the roads and stamp out corruption are immediately forgotten. These new democratic leaders end up with fabulous wealth and isolate themselves from the disease-stricken and downtrodden population. It is this situation which forces poor people to turn to Islam, which is now the fastest growing religion in the world, especially in Africa.

WORLD PROBLEMS ARRIVE IN DOVER

Thanks largely to the godless activities of their governments, life in most countries outside Europe and the United States is now so ghastly and poverty-stricken that it is hardly any wonder the populations are creeping into the East Kent coast on rubber dinghies. I am talking about yet another intractable and insoluble problem, only this one is right on my doorstep as I live in Dover. The morally bankrupt and futile western foreign policies have produced hordes of refugees, many of whom are now wandering along the motorways of East Kent in their faded tracksuits. Some politicians admit that the immigration problem has been the result of years of foreign policy failures, and indeed it has! But here comes the rub: some maintain that we must intervene more in these failed countries in order to make conditions pleasant enough to deter their citizens from leaving. I think even King Edward III would find such reasoning utterly distasteful. The strife which we westerners have caused in far-off countries about which we know nothing is the big chicken which is coming home to roost. And what can our politicians do about the immigration problem? Nothing, of course, because of all hot potatoes, this issue is the hottest.

In any case, what possible grounds can there be to ban immigrants? "To protect our British values," we hear. What values are they? Warm beer? Love of the underdog? Cricket? Everything which makes us British has now been squandered. The main thing which we have disposed of is God, and we have put in His place life without God. Now that we live in what has been termed the post-Christian era, the results are plain to see, if only we are prepared to look. The social cataclysm into which we are descending as a society is a symptom of a far deeper malaise, and that malaise is the attempt to have "good without God." The first cause of the destruction of our beloved country is the abandonment of commonly held moral and religious principles. Nobody knows why they should be good anymore. Besides, they ask, what does good even mean?

In this way, our country is not really a country anymore; it is more like an animal reservation which is populated largely by humans with two legs and two arms but who live, more or less, on their instincts, much like a flock of sheep. These instincts, such as "I'm too cold, I'm too hot, I'm hungry, I want a beer," are the basic principles governing modern society. We have nothing worth defending, so why *not* let in the immigrants—the Russians, or the Muslims? If one accepts these criticisms as an accurate portrayal of so-called "life in the West," then what right have any of us to interfere in the affairs of other countries and what exactly is it that we can offer them? I am certain that the poor residents of Baghdad look back fondly on the Saddam Hussein years as they observe the US-led destruction of their country.

This leads to a question which goes to the heart of the matter: can we sit on the sidelines whilst appalling atrocities are carried out in other countries which cry out to us for help? There are so many examples of this, such as the Balkans which suffered ethnic cleansing in the 1990s, Iraq, Afghanistan, Rwanda—the list is endless. The answer is not that easy when there is such a public outcry demanding that our government "do something." In most of these cases our intervention has either failed to stop the massacres or made matters far worse, as in Iraq. Even when we honoured our obligations to Poland in 1939 and declared war, that did not save that unhappy country from joint occupation by the Germans and the Russians.

SO, WHAT'S THE ANSWER?

Most of the problems in the world at large are of a supernatural origin and we know this because they are humanly insoluble. These difficulties are sent by God to bring us to our knees, that we may worship Him in the way He has demanded. More and more people are fast losing confidence in the ability of governments and politicians to sort out the mess, but they are not turning to the Church, far from it. Our mission, as Catholics, is to stop these people from running to extreme organisations, such as Islam and Communism. The Catholic Church is perfectly placed to sort out all these problems but, as we know, our Church leaders are part of the problem, not the solution, as they take the lead in adopting the ideals of the secular state. No, we have to repeat the age-old methods of our ancestors, which is to convert ourselves, our families, our loved ones, our neighbours, our towns, and finally, our countries. Then we can have real peace based on tranquillity. "Impossible!," you reply. Humanly speaking, yes. But with God on our side, we cannot fail and, in any case, everything we have tried up until now has utterly failed.

Cum placuerint Domino viae hominis,
inimicos quoque ejus convertet ad pacem.

"When a man's ways please the LORD, he makes even his enemies to be at peace with him" (Proverbs 16:7).

EPILOGUE

IT'S NOT ALL DOOM AND GLOOM!

I would not like to leave the reader with the impression that everything is black, with no possibility of improvement. I am definitely not someone who prays that Almighty God will pull the rug from under us and call a halt to world history. "Doomsayers" or "Armageddonists" look with relish on developing world events and are comforted that the end is not long in coming. I know people who stockpile blessed candles, blankets, and other emergency supplies, as they look for signs of the end of the world. I am not one of those people.

It must be admitted, however, that things couldn't be worse! The social collapse of our society is a fact which cries out from all corners of the earth. Here, in Dover, we are yards from two secondary schools and when I see the poor children emerging into the street after the end of the school day, I cannot fail to notice how miserable they all look. I suggest that you, the reader, take a walk round your local shopping mall. You will notice how the crowds mill around with sunken shoulders, almost like citizens of a defeated nation. Walking down Park Avenue in the mid-afternoon, I catch the following conversation between two girls:

"Yeah, Dad has cleared off with his new girlfriend."
"So, it's just Mum at home now?"

"Oh no, my new stepdad has already moved in, he's got two kids of his own and I don't know where they're going to sleep."

I am also aware of one of my relations who has invited a man friend to join him and his wife in an "open marriage." We have several acquaintances who live as homosexual couples. To demonstrate personal animosity towards them would be sinful and un-Catholic; however, if one must not hate the sinner, one must certainly always hate the sin. Although I have a few friends who are "gay," I am careful not to acknowledge their sinful relationship by inviting them over as a couple or, indeed, attending a "gay" event such as a wedding anniversary. The good thing is that my few "gay" friends know exactly what I, as a Catholic, believe about homosexuality and they good-naturedly avoid confronting me with their vice. When, rarely, they ask me about the Church's teachings on that subject, I take the opportunity to let rip. "Does that mean that we're going to hell?," one of them asks. The answer to that is: "Objectively speaking, yes!" We cannot know or judge their individual circumstances or the state of their souls, however, so we have to leave them to the justice and mercy of God.

If I restricted my circle of friends to Catholics who I believe are in a state of grace, their number would be very small indeed. Many Catholics and non-Catholics we know have cemented themselves into a state of mortal sin by cohabiting when already married to someone else. This is very common indeed. I have to be realistic and deal with such people as I find them. Having such a large number of brothers and sisters, nieces and nephews (over sixty in all), I am sometimes invited to celebrations which I find morally questionable. Usually I am spared these invitations, but awkward moments inevitably arise. I feel miserable about some of the things my relatives do, and hope and pray that they will convert. I know that the happiness which they are seeking through their actions will not arrive, as serious sin just increases our misery. "Happiness" is an inner tranquillity which can only be arrived at, as St Augustine says, through union with Christ. There are many pleasures which are perfectly healthy and legitimate, but the search for pleasure for its own sake is doomed to failure, as people who manage their lives purely for pleasure will know, deep down. Many years ago, a priest once told me: "If you wish to be truly happy, renounce all pleasures!"

I do not believe, in spite of the above, that God is so fed up with us that He will bring on a nuclear war. Above all, I do not think that God wants us to be miserable, and he definitely wants us to be with Him in heaven. There is always hope—miracles can and do happen. The point being, we cannot change the world for the better, any more than we are able to turn the clocks back. We are long past that now. God knows the solution to mankind's moral dissolution and will perform great works of mercy to put things right. All we do is get in His way by dreaming up our own solutions to the obvious problems. We are long past the time when we can make any material difference to the evils of the world. Politicians, faced with this situation, are unable to make a difference as they are themselves part of the problem, relying as they do on the notion of "good without God." We have to rely on God by obeying His precepts and not erect barriers to His grace. What other solution can there possibly be?

I will repeat the marvellous words of Evelyn Waugh, summarizing St Edmund Campion's boast: "The Faith is absolutely satisfactory to the mind, enlisting all knowledge and reason in its cause.... It is completely compelling to any who give it an 'indifferent and quiet audience.'"

AMDG